Anna Brownell Jameson

WINTER STUDIES AND SUMMER RAMBLES IN CANADA

Selections

Introduction : Clara Thomas
General Editor : Malcolm Ross
New Canadian Library N. 46

MCCLELLAND AND STEWART

First published in 1838 by Saunders and Ottley, London

ISBN 0-7710-9255-5

The Canadian Publishers
McClelland and Stewart Limited
25 Hollinger Road, Toronto

NOTE ON THE TEXT

The present abridged edition, first printed in 1965, follows the text of the 1839 edition (New York, Wiley & Putnam). No changes have been made in spelling and usage.

Manufactured in Canada by Webcom Limited

CONTENTS

INTRODUCTION

Though Canadian interest in Anna Jameson begins and often ends with *Winter Studies and Summer Rambles in Canada,* this book is only one of a long and diversified list of works by an author who was a considerable literary figure and arbiter of taste for nineteenth-century reading publics in England and America.

Twice before its publication in 1838, Mrs. Jameson had successfully used the travel-diary form with the author as heroine. In *Diary of an Ennuyée,* 1826, her first published work, she had adopted the mask of a broken-hearted young girl to record a trip taken through Europe in the company of a family for whom she was governess. In 1834, *Visits and Sketches at Home and Abroad* recorded another European tour, this time in the company of her father, Denis Murphy, a talented but financially unsuccessful miniature painter, and Sir Gerard Nöel, a wealthy patron and benefactor.

Mrs. Jameson's literary reputation was enhanced in England and particularly in Germany, by the publication of *Characteristics of Women* in 1833. This book, a series of critical sketches of Shakespeare's heroines, was reprinted many times. It was immediately translated into German and Mrs. Jameson's lengthy visit to Germany in 1834–35 had something of the quality of a triumphal tour. She was lionized and fêted wherever she went and she formed a lasting friendship with Ottilie von Goethe, the daughter-in-law of the poet. It was this trip which made Germany, its life and its literature one of the lasting interests of her life and one which is evinced in the pages of *Winter Studies.*

In 1825, Anna Murphy had married Robert Jameson, a young barrister with bright prospects, protégé of Lord Chancellor Eldon and, through his friendship with Hartley Coleridge, an acquaintance of many of London's literary men. In spite of Jameson's encouragement and patronage of his wife's early work, her many misgivings about their compatibility, recorded in letters during their three years of courtship, proved true. From its early days, their marriage was an unhappy one.

In 1829 Robert Jameson accepted a legal post in Dominica, and in 1833 he came to Upper Canada, this time to the considerable position of Attorney General. Anna Jameson came to Canada in 1836, partly from a sense of duty and a desire to give his new home and household the appearance of conventional normalcy during the months preceding his appointment in February 1837 as Vice-Chancellor, Upper Canada's highest legal position. She came, however, with little hope of mending a hopeless marriage or of staying permanently in Canada. When she left, some nine months after her arrival, it was with an agreement from her husband to an amicable separation, an allowance and, most important to her readers then and now, with a book well in the making.

And over that same door was likewise writ
Be bold, Be bold, and everywhere be bold;
That much she mused and yet could not construe it
By any riddling skill or common wit;
At last she spied at that room's upper end
Another iron door, on which was writ,
Be not too bold.

(Faerie Queene, Book III)

This was the epigraph carried by the first three-volume edition of *Winter Studies and Summer Rambles in Canada*, published in London by Saunders and Ottley, November 1838. It was a particularly apt one, considering that the text was in large part a personal account of Anna Jameson's stay in Upper Canada from December 1836 to late August or early September 1837, while the rebellion was gathering momentum for its December climax. Moreover, the account published was by the "Chancellor's Lady," the courtesy address which Mrs. Jameson reports with some satisfaction.

The line was a delicate one, therefore, between a frank, truthful, saleable account and one which might hurt her husband's reputation by its ill-considered remarks or, even more serious since she had given up her marriage, reflect upon her reputation by its bad taste. With the skill of one who was a veteran in tactful writing, Anna Jameson managed to tread the line, producing a work which is completely personal, impressive for the freshness of its tone and the exactness of its detail, at the same time insisting on her own complete responsibility for the opinions she expressed.

Much of the charm to her reading audience, accustomed to her combination of travel memoirs with social and literary criticism, would lie in the fact that in this book, too, she continued to use her familiar technique. The "Winter Studies" section is a journal of her winter stay in Toronto, interspersed with translations and commentaries from German works she was studying and with a new set of variations on her old theme: the character, position, and necessary education of women. "Summer Rambles," the account of a really impressive and unprecedented tour of Upper Canada, is also spiced with carefully chosen and well-authenticated Indian lore and, again, is written with a constant stress on the position of women among white settlers and Indians.

The trip began with her removal from Toronto to Niagara between June 10 and 13 of 1837. It ended with her return to Toronto on or about August 13: "At three o'clock in the morning, just as the moon was setting in Lake Ontario, I arrived at the door of my own house in Toronto, having been absent on this wild expedition just two months."

From Toronto to Niagara, Hamilton, Brantford, Woodstock, London, St. Thomas, Port Talbot, Chatham, and Detroit engaged the first month of the tour; though arduous, it could not be classed as a "wild expedition" in the way that her second month's travels could. Leaving Detroit on July 19, she went by the steamer *Jefferson* to Mackinaw, still well within reach of any eager traveller. From there, however, she travelled ninety-four miles by "bateau" (a small boat which held at most fifteen persons and which was rowed by five French-Canadian voyageurs) to the Sault, arriving there on July 29. On August 1, again in a bateau, she embarked for the annual Indian conclave at Manitoulin Island, a journey down Lake Huron of four days and three nights. On August 6, she continued by canoe to Penetang, by canoe and portage to Lake Simcoe, thence to Toronto. This latter half of her travels may indeed be dignified by the name of a "wild expedition" and in its successful completion, Anna Jameson took a very justifiable pride.

In "Winter Studies" particularly, the juxtaposition of her own cold and unhappy present surroundings with her German studies, an outgrowth of the cosmopolitan European civilization to which she was accustomed, keeps the author emphatically centre-stage, gallantly insisting on her own ideals of culture even with the temperature at twelve below zero and the ink frozen in her inkwell. Similarly, though the "Summer Rambles" section contains much that is interesting and informative, both now and then, it is the author as the heroine of the trip that is its chief attraction, differentiating it from many informative and colourful, but less well-dramatized travel diaries.

We recognize in Anna Jameson's writing method a three-part scheme. She read before travelling, in this case giving particular credit to Alexander Henry for having helped direct the course of her "Summer Rambles." She took notes and kept journals while travelling, these forming the core and the personalized part of her work. Finally, she edited and judiciously added supplementary material, as exact as possible in its detail, ranging from a lengthy history of Pontiac to the most minute details of Indian life and lore.

Her procedures were a combination of careful research and astute book-making, not quite exact scholarship as we know it today, but work which was documented and authenticated beyond the demands of either critics or public in her day. I can find no instance of a reviewer encouraging a more exact reference method by referring to its absence, though a commonplace of the reviews about Anna Jameson's work was their complimentary references to the exactness and apparent validity of her observation. Henry Schoolcraft, whose reputation as an authority on Indian life was an established one in his own day and is even more firmly fixed in ours, in spite of reservations about the authors who visited him at Michilimackinac, attributed to Anna Jameson "the most accurate and artistic eye of all." In a letter to George MacMurray, Anglican missionary to the Sault, requesting a variety of information subsequent to her stay there, the author herself spoke, with a confidence in the validity of her methods and the success of her enterprise which may have seemed intimidating to him but is delightful to us: "You must be content to be immortalized in my fashion."

The value of the "Summer Rambles" as a keenly observant early Canadian travel account is attested by its modern reprints. As well as the McClelland and Steward edition of 1923 and the Nelson edition of 1943, edited by James J. Talman and Elsie McLeod Murray, Gerald Craig has included selections from the Canadian tour in his *Early Travellers in the Canadas, 1791–1867*, 1955.

Anna Jameson's words have been used as authoritative illustration by many authors specializing in historical or biographical study. Ermatinger's use of her material in *The Talbot Régime*, Fred Landon's in *Lake Huron* and Chase and Stellanova Osborn's in *Schoolcraft–Longfellow–Hiawatha* all give evidence of the regard in which her observations are held. In each case, the editors have considered the work for its backward glance at life in early Canada and have, understandably, printed no part of the German material, the actual "Winter Studies."

The present edition, comprising about one-third of the original work, has, of necessity, omitted much and once again, almost all of the German studies. The selections have been made, however, with a view to giving the reader the flavour of Anna Jameson's entire work, not just skipping from place to place to provide a bare-bones itinerary of the Canadian tour, but including passages of considerable length. For example, certain of her passages considering the position of women in pioneer and in savage life have been included. The "woman question" was one of the preoccupations of all of her writing and, reasonable, even conservative, as her remarks seem to us, this facet of *Winter Studies and Summer Rambles* drew more critical comment than did any other aspect of the work.

Of the reviews, she reports to a friend: "Mrs. Procter writes to me that the book is universally relished and says 'a fig for reviewers'. The men, she says, are much alarmed by certain speculations about women; and, she adds, well they may be, for when the horse and ass begin to think and argue, adieu to riding and driving."

Winter Studies and Summer Rambles in Canada brought Anna Jameson a heightened success in both England and America where it was published early in 1839. Mr. Jameson is reported by his wife as being "much displeased" and on the whole, one does not wonder. What his Canadian compatriots thought of it, we do not know; if they read it, they left no comment. But it is safe to say that present-day Canadians can enjoy the tartness and precision of Anna Jameson's comment and relish her intrepidity, echoing the friend who wrote in appreciation: "You make the reader . . . live along with yourself, and an excellent companion we find you."

CLARA THOMAS

York University,
Toronto, Ontario.

WINTER STUDIES IN CANADA

Sind denn die Bäume auch so trostlos,
so verzweiflungs voll in ihrem Winter,
wie das Herz in seiner Verlassenheit?

Bettine v. Arnim

Dec. 20th.

TORONTO—such is now the sonorous name of this our sublime capital—was, thirty years ago, a wilderness, the haunt of the bear and deer, with a little ugly, inefficient fort, which, however, could not be more ugly or inefficient than the present one. Ten years ago Toronto was a village, with one brick house and four or five hundred inhabitants; five year ago it became a city, containing about five thousand inhabitants, and then bore the name of Little York; now it is Toronto, with an increasing trade, and a population of ten thousand people. So far I write as *per* book.

What Toronto may be in summer, I cannot tell; they say it is a pretty place. At present its appearance to me, a stranger, is most strangely mean and melancholy. A little ill-built town on low land, at the bottom of a frozen bay, with one very ugly church, without tower or steeple; some government offices, built of staring red brick, in the most tasteless, vulgar style imaginable; three feet of snow all around; and the gray, sullen, wintry lake, and the dark gloom of the pine forest bounding the prospect; such seems Toronto to me now. I did not expect much; but for this I was not prepared. Perhaps no preparation could have *prepared* me, or softened my present feelings. I will not be unjust if I can help it, nor querulous. If I look into my own heart, I find that it is regret for what I have left and lost—the absent, not the present—which throws over all around me a chill, colder than that of the wintry day—a gloom, deeper than that of the wintry night.

This is all very dismal, very weak, perhaps; but I know no better way of coming at the truth, than by observing and recording faithfully the impressions made by objects and characters on my own mind—or, rather, the impress they *receive* from my own mind—shadowed by the clouds which pass over its horizon, taking each tincture of its varying mood—until they emerge into light, to be corrected, or at least modified, by observation and comparison. Neither do I know any better way than this of conveying to the mind of another, the truth, and nothing but the truth, if not the whole truth. So I shall write on. Hitherto I have not been accused of looking on the things of this world through a glass darkly, but rather of a contrary tendency. What have I done with my spectacles *couleur de rose?*—the cheerful faith which sustained my through far worse than any thing I can anticipate here;—the desire to know, the impatience to learn, the quick social sympathies, the readiness to please and to be pleased—derived, perhaps, from my Irish blood, and to which I have owed so much of comfort when I have most needed it, so much of enjoyment when least I could have hoped for it—what! and are all forgotten, all gone? Yet am I not quite an icicle, nor an oyster—I almost wish I were! No, worst of all, is this regretful remembrance of friends who loved me, this heart-sick longing after home, and country, and all familiar things and dear domestic faces! I am like an uprooted tree, dying at the core, yet with a strange unreasonable power at times of mocking at my own most miserable weakness. Going to bed in tears last night, after saying my prayers for those far away across that terrible Atlantic, an odd remembrance flashed across me of that Madame de Boufflers, who declared "*avec tant de sérieux et de sentiment*," that she would consent to go as ambassadress to England, only on the condition of taking with her "*vingt-cinq ou vingt-six de ses amis intimes*," and sixty or eighty persons who were *absolument necessaires à son bonheur*. The image of graceful impertinence thus conjured up, made me smile—but am I so unlike her in this fit of unreason? Every where there is occupation for the rational and healthy intellect, every where good to be done, duties to be performed—every where the mind is, or should be, its own world, its own country, its own home at least. How many fine things I could say or quote, in prose or in rhyme, on this subject! But in vain I conjure up Philosophy, "she will not come when I do call for her;" but in her stead come thronging sad and sorrowful recollections, and shivering sensations, all telling me that I am a stranger among strangers, miserable inwardly and outwardly—and that the thermometer is twelve degrees below zero!

There is much, too, in first impressions, and as yet I have not recovered from the pain and annoyance of my outset here. My friends at New-York expended much eloquence—eloquence wasted in vain!—in endeavouring to dissuade me from a winter journey to Canada. I listened, and was grateful for their solicitude, but must own I did not credit the picture they drew of the difficulties and *désagrémens* I was destined to meet by the way. I had chosen, they said, (Heaven knows I did not *choose* it,) the very worst season for a journey through the state of New-York; the usual facilities for travelling were now suspended; a few weeks sooner the rivers and canals had been open; a few weeks later the roads, smoothed up with snow, had been in sleighing order; now, the navigation was frozen, and the roads so broken up as to be nearly impassable. Then there was only a night boat on the Hudson, "to proceed," as the printed paper set forth, "to Albany, *or as far as the ice permitted.*" All this, and more, were represented to me—and with so much apparent reason and real feeling, and in words and tones so difficult to resist! But though I could appreciate the kindness of those persuasive words, they brought no definite idea to my mind; I could form no notion of difficulties which by fair words, presence of mind, and money in my pocket, could not be obviated. I had travelled half over the continent of Europe, often alone, and had never yet been in circumstances where these availed not. In my ignorance I could conceive none; but I would not lightly counsel a similar journey to any one—certainly not to a woman.

As we ascended the Hudson in the night, I lost, of course, the view of that superb scenery which I was assured even winter could not divest of all its beauty—rather clothed it in a different kind of beauty. At the very first blush of morning, I escaped from the heated cabin, crowded with listless women and clamorous children, and found my way to the deck. I was surprised by a spectacle as beautiful as it was new to me. The Catskill mountains which we had left behind us in the night, were still visible, but just melting from the view, robed in a misty purple light, while our magnificent steamer—the prow armed with a sharp iron sheath for the purpose—was *crashing* its way through solid ice four inches thick, which seemed to close behind us into an adhesive mass, so that the wake of the vessel was not distinguished a few yards from the stern: yet in the path thus opened, and only seemingly closed, followed at some little distance a beautiful schooner and two smaller steam-vessels. I walked up and down, from the prow to the stern, refreshed by the keen frosty air, and the excitement caused by various picturesque effects, on the ice-bound river and the frozen shores, till we reached Hudson. Beyond this town it was not safe for the boat to advance, and we were still thirty miles below Albany. After leaving Hudson (with the exception of the rail-road between Albany and Utica,) it was all heavy, weary work; the most painfully fatiguing journey I ever remember. Such were the roads, that we were once six hours going eleven miles. What was usually a day's journey from one town, or one good inn to another, occupied sometimes a day and a night, or even two days.

One dark night, I remember, as the sleet and rain were falling fast and our Extra was slowly dragged by wretched brutes of horses through what seemed to me "sloughs of despond," some package ill stowed on the roof, which in the American stages presents no resting-place either for man or box, fell off. The driver alighted to fish it out of the mud. As there was some delay, a gentleman seated opposite to me put his head out of the window to inquire the cause; to whom the driver's voice replied in an angry tone: "I say you, mister, don't you sit jabbering there, but lend a hand to heave these things aboard!" To my surprise, the gentleman did not appear struck by the insolence of this summons, but immediately jumped out and lent his assistance. This is merely the manner of the people; the driver intended no insolence, nor was it taken as such, and my fellow-travellers could not help laughing at my surprise.

After six days and three nights of this travelling, unrelieved by companionship, or interest of any kind, I began to sink with fatigue. The first thing that roused me was our arrival at the ferry of the Niagara river, at Queenston, about seven miles below the Falls. It was a dark night, and while our little boat was tossed in the eddying waters, and guided by a light to the opposite shore, we could distinctly hear the deep roar of the cataract, filling, and, as it seemed to me, shaking the atmosphere around us. That mighty cataract, the dream and vision of my childhood and youth, so near—yet unseen—making itself thus heard and felt—like Job's vision, consciously present, yet unrevealed and undiscerned! You may believe that I woke up very decidedly from my lethargy of weariness to listen to that mysterious voice, which made my blood pause and thrill. At Queenston we slept, and proceeded next morning to the town of

Niagara on the shore of Lake Ontario. Now, as we had heard, the navigation on the lake had ceased, and we looked for nothing better than a further journey of one hundred miles round the head of the lake, and by the most execrable roads, instead of an easy passage of thirty miles across from shore to shore. But Fortune, seized with one of those freaks which, when we meet them in books, we pronounce improbable and unnatural (and she has played me many such, some good, some bad), had ordered matters otherwise. A steam-vessel, making a last trip, had called accidentally at the port, and was just going off; the paddles were actually in motion as I and my baggage together were hurried—almost *flung*—on board. No sooner there, than I threw myself down in the cabin utterly overwhelmed with fatigue, and sank at once into a profound and dreamless sleep.

How long I slept I knew not: they roused me suddenly to tell me we were at Toronto, and, not very well able to stand, I hurried on deck. The wharf was utterly deserted, the arrival of the steam-boat being accidental and unexpected; and as I stepped out of the boat I sank ankle-deep into mud and ice. The day was intensely cold and damp; the sky lowered sulkily, laden with snow, which was just beginning to fall. Half-blinded by the sleet driven into my face and the tears which filled my eyes, I walked about a mile through a quarter of the town mean in appearance, not thickly inhabited, and to me, as yet, an unknown wilderness; and through dreary, miry ways, never much thronged, and now, by reason of the impending snow-storm, nearly solitary. I heard no voices, no quick foot-steps of men or children; I met no familiar face, no look of welcome. I was sad at heart as a woman could be—and these were the impressions, the feelings, with which I entered the house which was to be called my *home!*

There is some need—is there not?—that I allow time for these sullen, unkindly influences to melt from my mind and heart before I judge of what I behold around me. The house—only a temporary residence while another is building—is ill provided with defences against the cold, and altogether comfortless; it has the advantage of commanding one of the principal roads entering the town and a glimpse of the bay—but at present all objects wear one hue. Land is not distinguishable from water. I see nothing but snow heaped up against my windows, not only without but within; I hear no sound but the tinkling of sleigh-bells and the occasional lowing of a poor half-starved cow, that, standing up to the knees in a snow-drift, presents herself at the door of a wretched little shanty opposite, and supplicates for her small modicum of hay.

Dec. 27.

With regard to the society, I can as yet say nothing, having seen nothing of it. All the official gentlemen have called, and all the ladies have properly and politely left their cards: so yesterday, in a sleigh, well wrapped in furs and buffalo robes, I set out duly to return these visits. I learned something of the geography of the town—nothing of the people. Those whom I did see, looked somewhat formal and alarmed, but they may be very excellent people for all that. I returned trembling and shuddering, chilled outwardly and inwardly, for none of my fur defences prevailed against the frost and the current of icy air, through which we glided, or rather flew, along the smooth road.

The appearance of the town was much more cheerful than on my first landing, but still melancholy enough. There was little movement or animation; few people in the streets; some good shops and some brick houses, but the greater number of wood. The very different appearance of the town and bay in the summer season, the blueness of the water, the brightness of the verdure, the throng of vessels, the busy crowds along the piers, were often described to me, but without conveying to my mind any very definite or cheering picture. The very novelty of the scene before me, by strongly impressing my imagination, seemed to shut out all power of anticipation.

The choice of this site for the capital of the Upper Province was decided by the fine harbor, the only one between Burlington Bay and Cobourg, a distance of about a hundred and fifty miles. General Simcoe, the first governor after the division of the two provinces, and a man of great activity and energy of character, entertained the idea of founding a metropolis. At that time the head quarters of the government were at Niagara, then called Newark, on the opposite shore; but this was too near the frontiers to be a safe position. Nor is Toronto much safer: from its low situation, and the want of any commanding height in the neighborhood, it is nearly defenceless. In case of a war with America, a few boats sent from the opposite coast of New-York could easily lay the fort and town in ashes; and, in fact, during the last war, in 1813, such was the fate of both. But the same reasons which rendered the place indefensible to us, rendered it untenable for the enemy, and it was immediately evacuated. Another objection was, and *is*, the unhealthiness of its situation,—in a low swamp not yet wholly drained, and with large portions of uncleared land immediately round it: still the beauty and safety of the spacious harbor, and its central position about halfway between Lake Huron and the frontier line of Lower Canada, have fixed its rank as capital of the province and the seat of the legislature.

When the engineer, Bouchette, was sent by General Simcoe to survey the site (in 1793) it was a mere swamp, a tangled wilderness; the birch, the hemlock and the tamarac-trees were growing down to the water's edge, and even into the lake. I have been told that Toronto, the Indian appellation of the whole district, signifies *trees growing out of water*. Colonel Bouchette says, that at this time the only vestige of humanity for a hundred miles on every side, was one solitary wigwam on the shore, the dwelling of a few Missassagua Indians. Three years afterwards, when the Duc de Rochefoucauld was here, the infant metropolis consisted of a fort and twelve miserable log huts, the inhabitants of which, as the duke tells us, bore no good reputation. The town was, however, already marked out in streets running parallel with the shore of the bay for about two miles, and crossed by others at right angles. It is a pity that while they were about it, they did not follow the example of the Americans, in such cases, and make the principal streets of ample width; some hundred feet, or even furlongs, more or less, would have made little difference where the wild unowned forest extended, for all they knew, from the lake to the north pole—*now*, it would be so easy to amend the error. King-street, the principal street, looks narrow, and will look narrower when the houses are higher, better and more regularly built. I perceive that in laying out the *fashionable* or west-end of the city, they have avoided the same mistake. A wide space between the building lots and Lake Ontario has been reserved very properly as a road or esplanade, but I doubt whether even this be wide enough. One of the most curious and inexplicable phenomena connected with these immense inland seas is the gradual rise of the waters; and even within these few years, as I am informed, great part of the high bank has been washed away, and a carriage-road at the foot of it along the shore has been wholly covered. If this process goes on, and at the same rate, there must be a solid embankment, or quay, raised as a barrier against the encroaching waters, or the esplanade itself will in time disappear.

Thus much of knowledge I gained in the course of my cold drive—bitter cold it was every way, and I returned without being much comforted or edified by my visits.

New Year's Day—colder than ever. This morning the thermometer stood at eighteen degrees below zero, and Dr. R—— told me that some chemical compounds in his laboratory had frozen in the night, and burst the phials in which they were contained.

They have here at Toronto the custom which prevails in France, Germany, the United States (more or less every where, I believe, but in England), of paying visits of congratulation on the first day of the year. This custom, which does not apparently harmonize with the manners of the people, has been borrowed from the French inhabitants of Lower Canada.

I received this morning about thirty gentlemen—to gentlemen luckily for me the obligation is confined—two-thirds of whom I had never seen nor heard of before, nor was there any one to introduce them. Some of them, on being ushered into the room, bowed, sat down, and after the lapse of two minutes, rose and bowed themselves out of the room again without uttering a syllable; all were too much in a hurry and apparently far too cold to converse. Those who did speak, complained, sensibly enough, of the unmeaning duty imposed on them, and the danger incurred by running in and out from the over-heated rooms into the fierce biting air, and prophesied to themselves and others sore throats, the agues, and fevers, and every ill that flesh is heir to. I could but believe and condole.. These strange faces appeared and disappeared in succession so rapidly, that I was almost giddy, but there were one or two among the number, whom even in five minutes' conversation I distinguished at onces as superior to the rest, and original minded, thinking men.

In London society I met with many men whose real material of mind it was difficult to discover—either they had been smoothed and polished down by society, or education had overlaid their understanding with stuccoed ornaments, and figures historical and poetical—very pretty to look at—but the coarse brick-work or the rotten lath and plaster lay underneath; there being in this new country far less of conventional manner, it was so much easier to tell at once the brick from the granite and the marble.

Jan. 12.

We have had another considerable fall of snow, and the weather is milder. They say here that the weather never remains the same for more than three days together; and all agree that the atmospherical changes are violent and sudden at all seasons. Yet the medical men assure me that the climate of Canada, take it altogether, is one of the healthiest in the world, though the immediate vicinity of Toronto be for the present, from local circumstances, an exception. The winter in the upper province is infinitely less severe and trying that the same season in Lower Canada.

Jan. 14.

It should seem that this wintry season, which appears to me so dismal, is for the Canadians the season of festivity, and if I were not sick and a stranger—if I had friends near me, I should really enjoy it. Now is the time for visiting, for sleighing excursions, for all intercourse of business and friendship, for balls in town, and dances in farm-houses, and courtships and marriages, and prayer-meetings and assignation of all sorts. In summer, the heat and the mosquitoes render travelling disagreeable at best; in spring the roads are absolutely impassable; in autumn there is too much argricultural occupation; but in winter the forests are pervious; the roads present a smooth surface of dazzling snow; the settlers in the woods drive into the towns, supply themselves with stores and clothing, and fresh meat, the latter a luxury which they can seldom obtain in the summer. I stood at my window to-day watching the sleighs as they glided past. They are of all shapes and sizes. A few of the carriage-sleighs are well appointed and handsome. The market-sleighs are often two or three boards nailed together in the form of a wooden box upon runners; some straw and a buffalo skin or blanket serve for the seat; barrels of flour and baskets of eggs fill up the empty space. Others are like cars, and others, called *cutters*, are mounted on high runners, like sleigh phaetons; these are sported by the young men and officers of the garrison, and require no inconsiderable skill in driving; however, as I am assured, they are overturned in the snow not above once in a quarter of an hour, and no harm and much mirth ensues; but the wood sleighs are my delight: a large platform of boards is raised upon runners, with a few upright poles held together at top by a rope, the logs of oak, pine, and maple, are then heaped up to the height of six or seven feet. On the summit lie a couple of deer frozen stiff, their huge antlers projecting in a most picturesque fashion, and on these again, a man is seated with a blanket round him, his furred cap drawn down upon his ears, and his scarlet woollen comforter forming a fine bit of color. He guides with a pole his two patient oxen, the clouds of vapor curling from their nostrils into the keen frosty air—the whole machine, in short, as wildly picturesque as the grape wagons in Italy, though, to be sure, the associations are somewhat different.

Jan. 16.

This morning, before I was quite dressed a singular visit was announced. I had expressed to my friend Mr. Hepburne a wish to see some of the aborigines of the country; he had the kindness to remember my request, and Colonel Givins, the principal Indian agent, had accordingly brought some

Indians to visit us. Those to whom the appearance of these people is familiar and by no means interesting, were surprised by a curiosity which you will at least allow was very natural and *feminine.*

The party consisted of three—a chief named the White Deer, and two of his friends. The chief wore a blanket coat, and leggings, and a blanket hood with a peak from which depended a long black eagle plume; stout mocazins or shoes of undressed deer-skin completed his attire; he had about fifty strings of blue wampum round his neck. The other two were similarly dressed, with the exception of the wampum and the feathers. Before I went down I had thrown a chain of wampum round my neck, which seemed to please them. Chairs being presented, they sat down at once (though, as Colonel Givins said, they would certainly have preferred the floor), and answered with a grave and quiet dignity the compliments and questions addressed to them. Their deportment was taciturn and self-possessed, and their countenances melancholy; that of the chief was by far the most intelligent. They informed me that they were Chippewas from the neighborhood of Lake Huron; that the hunting season had been unsuccessful; that their tribe was suffering the extremity of hunger and cold; and that they had come to beg from their Great Father the Governor rations of food, and a supply of blankets for their women and children. They had walked over the snow, in their snow-shoes, from the lake, one hundred and eighty miles, and for the last forty-eight hours none of them had tasted food. A breakfast of cold meat, bread, and beer, was immediately ordered for them; and though they had certainly never beheld in their lives the arrangement of an European table, and were besides half-famished, they sat down with unembarrassed tranquillity, and helped themselves to what they wished, with the utmost propriety—only, after one or two trials, using their own knives and fingers in preference to the table knife and fork. After they had eaten and drunk sufficiently, they were conducted to the government-house to receive from the governor presents of blankets, rifles, and provisions, and each, on parting, held out his hand to me, and the chief, with grave earnestness, prayed for the blessing of the Great Spirit on me and my house. On the whole, the impression they left, though amusing and exciting from its mere novelty, was melancholy. The sort of desperate resignation in their swarthy countenances, their squalid, dingy habiliments, and their forlorn story, filled me with pity, and, I may add, disappointment; and all my previous impressions of the independent children of the forest are for the present disturbed.

These are the first specimens I have seen of that fated race, with which I hope to become better acquainted before I leave the country. Notwithstanding all I have heard and read, I have yet but a vague idea of the Indian character; and the very different aspect under which it has been represented by various travellers, as well as writers of fiction, adds to the difficulty of forming a correct estimate of the people, and more particularly of the true position of their women. Colonel Givins, who has passed thirty years of his life among the north-west tribes, till he has become in habits and language almost identified with them, is hardly an impartial judge. He was their interpreter on this occasion, and he says that there is as much difference between the customs and language of different nations, the Chippewas and Mohawks, for instance, as there is between any two nations of Europe.

January 16.

Some philosopher has said or written, that our good and bad qualities, our virtues and our vices, depend more on the influence of climate, than the pride of civilized humanity would be willing to allow; and this is a truth or truism, which for my own part I cannot gainsay—yet which I do not much like to believe. Whatever may be the climate in which the human being is born or reared, can he not always by moral strength raise himself above its degrading, or benumbing, or exciting influence? and yet more, rather than less, easily, when, at a mature age and with habits formed, he is subjected accidentally to such influences? Is there most wisdom, in such a case, in passively assimilating ourselves, our habits, and our feelings, to external circumstances, or resisting and combating them, rather to defend the integrity of our own individual being, than with the hope of changing or controlling the physical or social influences around us?

How I might have settled this question with myself, long ago, when in possession of the health and energy and trusting spirit of my young years, I know—but now it is too late. I could almost wish myself a dormouse, or a she-bear, to sleep away the rest of this cold, cold winter, and wake only with the first green leaves, the first warm breath of the summer wind. I shiver through the day and through the night; and, like poor Harry Gill, "my teeth they chatter, chatter still;" and then at intervals I am burned up with a dry hot fever: this is what my maid, a good little Oxfordshire girl, calls the *hager* (the ague), more properly the lake fever, or cold fever. From the particular situation of Toronto, the disorder is very prevalent here in the spring: being a stranger, and not yet *acclimatée*, it has attacked me thus unseasonably. Bark is the general and unfailing remedy.

The cold is at this time so intense, that the ink freezes while I write, and my fingers stiffen round the pen; a glass of water by my bed-side, within a few feet of the hearth (heaped with logs of oak and maple kept burning all night long), is a solid mass of ice in the morning. God help the poor emigrants who are yet unprepared against the rigor of the season!—yet this is nothing to the climate of the lower province, where, as we hear, the thermometer has been thirty degrees below zero. I lose all heart to write home, or to register a reflection or a feeling;—thought stagnates in my head as the ink in my pen—and this will never do!—I *must* rouse myself to occupation; and if I cannot find it without, I must create it from within. There are yet four months of winter and leisure to be disposed of. How?—I know not; but they *must* be employed, not wholly lost.

The House of Assembly is now sitting, and the question at present agitated is the appropriation of the clergy reserves—a question momentous to the future welfare of the colony, and interesting to every thinking mind. There are great differences of opinion, and a good deal of bitterness of spirit, prevailing on this subject, so often brought under discussion, and as yet unsettled. When Upper Canada was separated from the Lower Province (in 1791) one-seventh part of the lands was set apart for the maintenance of the clergy, under the name of Clergy Reserves; and the Church of England, as being the church by law established, claimed the entire appropriation of these lands. The Roman Catholics, under the old conditions by which the maintenance of their church was provided for on the conquest of the colony, also put in their claim, as did the Presbyterians on account of their influence, and the Methodists on account of their number. The inhabitants, meantime, through the legislature, petitioned the government that the whole of the clergy reserves should be appropriated to the purposes of education, for which the funds already provided are wholly inadequate, and are ill managed besides—but of this hereafter. If the question had been left to be settled by the House of Assembly then sitting, the Radicals of 1832, there is no doubt that such would have been the destination of these reserves, which now consist of about two millions of acres out of fourteen millions, settled or in course of cultivation, and indefinitely increasing as more and more land is redeemed from the unmeasured, interminable forest. The government at home sent over to the legislature here a cession of the crown lands, and a recommendation to settle the whole question; but we have now a House of Assembly differently constituted from that of 1832, and the preponderance is altogether the other way. I am now aware that there exist three parties on this subject:

First, those who would appropriate the whole of these reserves solely to the maintenance of the Church of England. This is a small but zealous party—not so much insisting on their own claim, as on the absolute inconsistency and unrighteousness of allowing any other claim. The Church of England, as the archdeacon observed last night, being the only true church, as well as the church by law established, to maintain any other religion or form of religion, at the expense of the state, is a manifest rebellion against both the *gospel* and the *law*.

A second party represent that the Church of England consists of but a small number of the colonists; that as no profession of belief (Quakerism excepted) can exclude a man from the provincial legislature, so each religion tolerated by the state should be by the state maintained. They exclaim against disuniting religion and education, and insist that the reserves should be divided in shares proportionate to the number of members of each church—among the Episcopalians, Presbyterians, Roman Catholics, Wesleyan Methodists, and Baptists. This party is numerous, but not unanimous. In hostility to the exclusive pretensions of the episcopal church they are agreed, but they seem to agree in nothing else; and some numerous and respectable sects are altogether excluded.

A third party, and by far the most numerous, require that the maintenance of the clergy should be left, as in the United States, to the voluntary aid of their congregation, and the entire produce of the lands reserved for the education of the people.

I have not been long enough in the country to consider the question practically, as applying to the peculiar wants and circumstances of the people; but theoretically I do not agree with any of these parties, and at present am content to listen to all I hear around me. With regard to the petition forwarded to the home government, it has been an ample source of ridicule that a house of parliament, of which many members could not read, and many more could not spell, should be thus zealous on the subject of education. In truth, I have seen some specimens of the writing and spelling of honorable members, men of influence and property too, at which it was impossible not to laugh; but I felt no disposition to join in the ridicule freely bestowed on the writers: it seemed any thing but ridiculous, that men who had not themselves received the advantage of a good education, should be anxious to insure it to their children. Mr. H. told me the other day, that in the distant townships not one person in twenty or thirty could read or write, or had the means of attaining such knowledge. On repeating this to Mr. B., a native Canadian, and perfectly acquainted with the country, adding some expression of incredulity, he exclaimed, laughing, "Not one in twenty or thirty!—Madam, not one in seventy!"

The question, as a mere party question, did not interest me; but the strange, crude, ignorant, vague opinions I heard in conversation, and read in the debates and the provincial papers, excited my astonishment. It struck me that if I could get the English preface to Victor Cousin's report (of which I had a copy) printed in a cheap form, and circulated with the newspapers, adding some of the statistical calculations, and some passages from Duppa's report on the education of the children of the poorer classes, it might do some good—it might assist the people to some general principles on which to form opinions; whereas they all appeared to me astray, nothing that had been promulgated in Europe on this momentous subject had yet reached them; and the brevity and clearness of this little preface, which exhibits the importance of a system of national education, and some general truths without admixture of any political or sectarian bias, would, I thought—I hoped—obtain for it a favorable reception. But, no; cold water was thrown upon me from every side—my interference in any way was so visibly distasteful, that I gave my project up with many a sigh, and I am afraid I shall always regret this. True, I am yet a stranger—helpless as to means, and *feeling* my way in a social system of which I know little or nothing; perhaps I might have done more mischief than good—who knows? and truth is sure to prevail at last; but truth seems to find so much difficulty in crossing the Atlantic, that one would think she was "like the poor cat i' the adage," afraid of wetting her feet.

Another fit of illness and fever of four days' duration happily over; but it has left me more good-for-nothing than ever—more dejected and weak.

Mr. Campbell, the clerk of the assize, has politely offered to drive me over to Niagara in his sleigh. Good-natured Mr. Campbell! I never saw the man in my life; but, in the excess of my gratitude, am ready to believe him every thing that is delightful; my heart was dying within me, gasping and panting for change of some kind—any kind! I suppose from the same sort of instinct which sends the wounded animal into the forest to seek for the herb which shall heal him. For here is Dr. R., who assures me that change of air is the only thing which can counteract the effect of these successive fits of aguish fever: so it is fixed that on Tuesday next, at eight o'clock in the morning, I shall be ready to step into Mr. Campbell's sleigh. Five days—five times twenty-four hours of frost and snow without, and monotonous solitude within—and my faculties, and my fingers, and my ink, all frozen up!

"So slow the unprofitable moments roll,
That lock up all the functions of my soul,
That keep me from myself."

Slow?—yes; but why unprofitable? that were surely my own fault!

❧

January 21.

There is some diminution of the intense cold yesterday and to-day. The thermometer is above zero.

I begin to be ashamed of recording idle days and useless days, and to have a conception of what those unfortunate wretches must suffer, who are habitually without an interest and without an occupation. What a life is this!

> "Life which the very stars reprove,
> As on their silent tasks they move."

To me it is something new, for I have never yet been *ennuyée to death*—except in fiction. It is like the old-fashioned torture patronized by that amiable person, Queen Elizabeth, when a certain weight was placed on the bosom of the criminal, and increased gradually every day till the life and the heart were crushed together. Well! patience and resignation are still at hand:—but Patience, "the young and rose-lipped cherubim," seems to have borrowed the features of grim Necessity, and, instead of singing an angel's song, clanks her fetters in my ear; and Resignation comes in a form which reminds me of Ottilie's definition—"Resignation, my dear, is only a despair, which does not beat people." Yet there remains DUTY, which is, far more than Love—

> . . . "The star to every wandering bark,
> That looks on tempests, and is never shaken."

It is the upholding law through which the weakest become strong, without which all strength is unstable as water. No character, however harmoniously framed and gloriously gifted, can be complete without this abiding principle; it is the cement which binds the whole moral edifice together, without which all power, goodness, intellect, truth, happiness, love itself, can have no permanence; but all the fabric of existence crumbles away from under us, and leaves us at last sitting in the midst of a ruin—astonished at our own desolation.

Merrily dash we o'er valley and hill,
All but the sleigh-bell is sleeping and still;
O bless the dear sleigh-bell! there's nought can compare
To its loud merry tones as they break on the ear.

Our horses are staunch, and they dash o'er the snow;
Our bells ring out gaily the faster we go;
The night breezes sing with an answering swell
To the melody rude of the merry sleigh-bell.

Canadian Song.

January 23.

At half-past eight Mr. Campbell was at the door in a very pretty commodious sleigh, in form like a barouche, with the head up. I was absolutely buried in furs; a blanket, netted for me by the kindest hands, of the finest lamb's-wool, rich in color, and as light and elastic as it was deliciously warm, was folded round my limbs; buffalo and bear-skins were heaped over all, and every breath of the external air excluded by every possible device. Mr. Campbell drove his own gray horses; and thus fortified and accoutred, off we flew, literally "urged by storms along the slippery way," for the weather was terrific.

I think that but for this journey I never could have imagined the sublime desolation of a northern winter, and it has impressed me strongly. In the first place, the whole atmosphere appeared as if converted into snow, which fell in thick, tiny, starry flakes, till the buffalo robes and furs about us appeared like swansdown, and the harness on the horses of the same delicate material. The whole earth was a white waste: the road, on which the sleigh-track was only just perceptible, ran for miles in a straight line; on each side rose the dark, melancholy pine-forest, slumbering drearily in the hazy air. Between us and the edge of the forest were frequent spaces of cleared or half-cleared land, spotted over with the black charred stumps and blasted trunks of once magnificent trees, projecting from the snowdrift. These, which are perpetually recurring objects in a Canadian landscape, have a most melancholy appearance. Sometimes wide openings occurred to the left, bringing us in sight of Lake Ontario, and even in some places down upon the edge of it: in this part of the lake the enormous body of the water and its incessant movement prevents it from freezing, and the dark waves rolled in, heavily plunging on the icy shore with a sullen booming sound. A few roods from the land, the cold gray waters, and the cold, gray, snow-encumbered atmosphere, were mingled with each other, and each seemed either. The only living thing I saw in a space of about twenty miles was a magnificent bald-headed eagle, which, after sailing a few turns in advance of us, alighted on the topmost bough of a blasted pine, and slowly folding his great wide wings, looked down upon us as we glided beneath him.

The first village we passed through was Springfield, on the river Credit, a river of some importance in summer, but now, converted into ice, heaped up with snow, and undistinguishable. Twenty miles further, we stopped at Oakville to refresh ourselves and the horses.

Oakville stands close upon the lake, at the mouth of a little river called Sixteen Mile Creek; it owes its existence to a gentleman of the name of Chisholm, and, from its situation and other local cicumstances, bids fair to become a place of importance. In the summer it is a frequented harbor, and carries on a considerable trade in *lumber*, for so they characteristically call timber in this country. From its dock-yards I am told that a fine steamboat and a dozen schooners have been already launched.

In summer, the country round is rich and beautiful, with a number of farms all in a high state of cultivation; but Canada in winter and in summer must be like two different regions. At present the mouth of the creek is frozen up; all trade, all ship-building suspended. Oakville presents the appearance of a straggling hamlet, containing a few frame and log-houses; one brick house (the grocery store, or general shop, which in a new Canadian village is always the best house in the place), a little Methodist church, painted green and white, but as yet no resident preacher; and an inn dignified by the name of the "Oakville House Hotel." Where there is a store, a tavern, and a church, habitations soon rise around them. Oakville contains at present more than three hundred inhabitants, who are now subscribing among themselves for a schoolmaster and a resident clergyman.

I stood conversing in the porch, and looking about me, till I found it necessary to seek shelter in the house, before my nose was absolutely taken off by the ice-blast. The little parlor was solitary, and heated like an oven. Against the wall were stuck a few vile prints, taken out of old American magazines; there was the Duchess de Berri in her wedding-dress, and as a pendant, the Modes de Paris—"Robe de tulle garnie de fleurs—coiffure nouvelle, inventée par Mons. Plaisir." The incongruity was but too laughable! I looked round me for some amusement or occupation, and at last spied a book open, and turned down upon its face. I pounced upon it as a prize; and what do you think it was? "Dévinez, madame! je vous le donne en trois, je vous le donne en quatre!" it was —Don Juan! And so, while looking from the window on a scene which realized all you can imagine of the desolation of savage life, mixed up with just so much of the common-place vulgarity of civilized life as sufficed to spoil it, I amused myself reading of the Lady Adéline Amundeville and her precious coterie, and there anent.

> Society is smoothed to that excess,
> That manners hardly differ more than dress.
> Our ridicules are kept in the back ground,
> Ridiculous enough, but also dull;
> Professions, too, are no more to be found
> Professional, and there is nought to cull
> Of Folly's fruit; for though your fools abound,
> They're barren, and not worth the pains to pull.
> Society is now one polished horde,
> Form'd of two mighty tribes—the *bores* and *bored*.

A delineation, by the way, which might almost reconcile one to a more savage locality than that around me.

While I was reading, the mail-coach between Hamilton and Toronto drove up to the door; and because you shall understand what sort of a thing a Canadian mail is, and thereupon sympathize in my irrepressible wonder and amusement, I must sketch it for you. It was a heavy wooden edifice, about the size and form of an old-fashioned lord mayor's coach, placed on runners, and raised about a foot from the ground; the whole was painted of a bright red, and long icicles hung from the roof. This monstrous machine disgorged from its portal eight men-creatures, all enveloped in bear-skins and shaggy dreadnoughts, and pea-jackets, and fur-caps down upon their noses, looking like a procession of bears on their hind-legs, tumbling out of a showman's caravan. They proved, however, when undisguised, to be gentlemen, most of them going up to Toronto to attend their duties in the House of Assembly. One of these, a personage of remarkable height and size, and a peculiar cast of features, was introduced to me as Mr. Kerr, the possessor of large estates in the neghborhood, partly acquired, and partly inherited from his father-in-law, Brandt, the famous chief of the Six Nations. Kerr himself has Indian blood in his veins. His son, young Kerr, a fine boy about ten years old, is the present acknowledged chief of the Six Nations, in his mother's right, the hereditary chieftainship being always transmitted *through* the female, though passing *over* her. Mrs. Kerr, the eldest daughter of Brandt, is a squaw of unmixed Indian blood, and has been described to me as a very superior creature. She has the good sense to wear habitually her Indian costume, slightly modified, in which she looks and moves a princess, graceful and unrestrained, while in a fashionable European dress the effect is exactly the reverse.

Much mischief has been done in this neighborhood by beasts of prey, and the deer, driven by hunger and the wolves from their forest haunts, have been killed, near the settlements, in unusual numbers. One of the Indians whom I saw at Toronto, on returning by this road, shot with his new rifle eight deer in one day, and sold them at Hamilton for three dollars each—no bad day's hunting. The venison in Canada is good and abundant, but very lean, very unlike English venison; the price is generally four or six cents (two pence or three pence) a pound.

After taking some refreshment, we set forth again. The next village we passed was called, oddly enough, Wellington Square; it has been recently laid out, and contains about twenty wooden houses; then came Port Nelson, Mr Kerr's place. Instead of going round the head of the lake by Hamilton, we crossed that very remarkable tongue or slip of land which divides Burlington Bay from Lake Ontario; these were, in fact, two separate lakes till a channel was cut through the narrow isthmus. Burlington Bay, containing about forty square miles, is now one sheet of ice, and on the slip of land, which is near seven miles in length, and about two hundred yards in width, we found the snow lying so deep and in such irregular drifts, that we proceeded with difficulty. At length we reached Stony Creek, a village celebrated in these parts as the scene of the bloodiest battle fought between the English and Americans during the last war. We had intended to sleep here, but the inn was so uncomfortable and unpromising, that after a short rest we determined on proceeding ten miles further to Beamsville.

It was now dark, and, the snow falling thick, it soon became impossible to distinguish the sleigh-track. Mr Campbell loosened the reins and left the horses to their own instinct, assuring me it was the safest way of proceeding. After this I remember no more distinctly, except that I ceased to hear the ever-jingling sleigh-bells. I awoke, as if from the influence of nightmare, to find the sleigh overturned, myself lying in the bottom of it half-smothered, and my companions nowhere to be seen; they were floundering in the snow behind.

Luckily, when we had stretched ourselves and shaken off the snow, we were found unhurt in life and limb. We had fallen down a bank into the bed of a rivulet, or a mill-race, I believe, which, being filled up with snow, was quite as soft, only a little colder, than a down-bed. Frightened I was, bewildered rather, but "effective" in a moment. It was impossible for the gentlemen to leave the horses, which were plunging furiously up to the shoulders in the snow, and had already broken the sleigh; so I set off to seek assistance, having received proper directions. Fortunately we were not far from Beamsville. My beacon-light was to be the chimney of a forge, from which the bright sparks were streaming up into the dark wintry air, visible from a great distance. After scrambling through many a snow-drift, up hill and down hill, I at last reached the forge, where a man was hammering amain at a ploughshare; such was the din, that I called for some time unheard; at last, as I advanced into the red light of the fire, the man's eyes fell upon me, and I shall never forget his look as he stood poising his hammer, with the most comical expression of bewildered amazement. I could not get an answer from him; he opened his mouth and repeated *aw!* staring at me, but without speaking or moving. I turned away in despair, yet half-laughing, and after some more scrambling up and down, I found myself in the village, and was directed to the inn. Assistance was immediately sent off to my friends, and in a few minutes the supper table was spread, a pile of logs higher than myself blazing away in the chimney; venison-steaks, and fried fish, coffee, hot cakes, cheese, and whiskey punch (the traveller's fare in Canada), were soon smoking on the table; our landlady presided, and the evening passed merrily away.

The old landlady of this inn amused me exceedingly; she had passed all her life among her equals in station and education, and had no idea of any distinction between guests and customers; and while caressing and attending on me, like an old mother or an old nurse, gave me her history, and that of all her kith and kin. Forty years before, her husband had emigrated, and built a hovel, and made a little clearing on the edge of the lake. At that time there was no other habitation within many miles of them, and they passed several years in almost absolute solitude. They have now three farms, some hundred acres of land, and have brought up nine sons and daughters, most of whom are married, and settled on lands of their own. She gave me a horrid picture of the prevalence of drunkenness, the vice and the curse of this country.

I can give you no idea of the intense cold of this night; I was obliged to wrap my fur cloak round me before I could go to sleep. I rose ill and could eat no breakfast, in spite of all the coaxing of the good landlady; she got out her best tea, kept for her own drinking (which tasted for all the world, like musty hay), and buttered toast, *i.e.* fried bread steeped in melted butter, and fruit preserved in molasses—to all which I shall get used in time—I must try, at least, or "thank Heaven, *fasting*." We proceeded eighteen miles further, to St. Catherine's, the situation of which appeared to me very pretty even in winter, and must be beautiful in summer. I am told it is a place of importance, owing to the vicinity of the Welland Canal, which connects Lake Ontario with Lake Erie: it contains more than seven hundred inhabitants. The school here is reckoned the best in the district. We passed this morning several streams, which in summer flow into the lake, now all frozen up and undistinguishable, except by the wooden bridges which cross them, and the mills, now still and useless, erected along their banks. These streams have the names of Thirty Mile Creek, Forty Mile Creek, Twenty Mile Creek, and so on; but wherefore I could not discover.

From St. Catherine's we proceeded twelve miles farther, to Niagara. There I found some old English or rather Irish friends ready to welcome me with joyous affection; and surely there is not a more blessed sight than the face of an old friend in a new land!

January 26.

The town of Niagara presents the same torpid appearance which seems to prevail every where at this season; it is situated at the mouth of the river Niagara, and is a place of much business and resort when the navigation is open. The lake does not freeze here, owing to the depth of its majestic waters; neither does the river, from the velocity of its current; yet both are blocked up by the huge fragments of ice which are brought down from Lake Erie, and which, uniting and accumulating at the mouth of the river, form a field of ice extending far into the lake. How beautiful it looked to-day, broken into vast longitudinal flakes of alternate white and azure, and sparkling in the sunshine!

There are dock-yards here lately erected, dry docks, iron works of some extent, and a steam-engine for hauling up vessels for repair; the chief proprietor is a good-natured and public-spirited gentleman, Captain Melville. He tells me that upwards of twenty thousand pounds have been expended on these works, and they employ constantly about fifty workmen; yet, in spite of this, and in spite of its local advantages, as a frontier town and the oldest settlement in Upper Canada, Niagara does not make progress. The population and the number of houses have remained nearly stationary for the last five years. I find the people complaining much of the want of a good school.

The land all around Niagara is particularly fine and fertile, and it has been longer cleared and cultivated than in other parts of the province. The country, they say, is most beautiful in summer, taxes are trifling, scarcely felt, and there are no poor-rates; yet ignorance, recklessness, despondancy, and inebriety, seem to prevail. A——, who has been settled here for five years, and B——, himself a Canadian, rate the morality of the Canadian population frightfully low; lying and drunkenness they spoke of as nearly universal; men who come here with sober habits quickly fall into the vice of the country; and those who have the least propensity to drinking find the means of gratification comparatively cheap, and little check from public opinion.

> Men learn to drink, who never drank before;
> And those who always drank, now drink the more.

Though I parody, I do not jest; for in truth, if all, or even half, of what I heard to-day be true, this is a horrible state of things. I asked for a bookseller's shop; there is not one in the town, but plenty of taverns. There is a duty of thirty per cent. on books important from the United States, and the expense on books imported from England adds at least one-third to their price; but there is no duty on whiskey. "If government," said B——, "were to lay a duty on whiskey, we should only have the province overrun with illicit stills, and another source of crime and depravity added to the main one."

Sir Francis Head recommended to me, playfully, to get up a grievance, that I might have an excuse for paying him a visit. I think I will represent to his Excellency the dearness of books and the cheapness of whiskey. I could not invent a worse grievance either in earnest or in jest.

The opposite shore, about a quarter of a mile off, is the State of New-York. The Americans have a fort on their side, and we also have a fort on ours. What the amount of *their* garrison may be I know not, but our force consists of three privates and a corporal, with adequate arms and ammunition, i.e. rusty firelocks and damaged guns. The fortress itself I mistook for a dilapidated brewery. This is charming—it *looks* like peace and security, at all events.

January 29.

Well! I have seen these cataracts of Niagara, which have thundered in my mind's ear ever since I can remember —which have been my "childhood's thought, my youth's desire," since first my imagination was awakened to wonder and to wish. I have beheld them, and shall I whisper it to you!—but, O tell it not among the Philistines—I wish I had not! I wish they were still a thing unbeheld—a thing to be imagined, hoped, and anticipated—something to live for:—the reality has displaced from my mind an illusion far more magnificent than itself—I have no words for my utter disappointment: yet I have not the presumption to suppose that all I have heard and read of Niagara is false of exaggerated—that every expression of astonishment, enthusiasm, rapture, is affectation or hyperbole. No! it must be my own fault. Terni, and some of the Swiss cataracts leaping from their mountains, have affected me a thousand times more than all the immensity of Niagara. O I could beat myself! and now there is no help!—the first moment, the first impression is over—is lost; though I should live a thousand years, long as Niagara itself shall roll, I can never see it again for the first time. Something is gone that cannot be restored. What has come over my soul and senses?—I am no longer Anna—I am metamorphosed—I am translated—I am an ass's head, a clod, a wooden spoon, a fat weed growing on Lethe's bank, a stock, a stone, a petrifaction—for have I not seen Niagara, the wonder of wonders; and felt—no words can tell *what* disappointment!

But, to take things in order: we set off for the Falls yesterday morning, with the intention of spending the day there, sleeping, and returning the next day to Niagara. The distance is fourteen miles, by a road winding along the banks of the Niagara river, and over the Queenston heights; and beautiful must this land be in summer, since even now it is beautiful. The flower garden, the trim shrubbery, the lawn, the meadow with its hedgerows, when frozen up and wrapt in snow, always give me the idea of something not only desolate but dead: Nature is the ghost of herself, and trails a spectral pall; I always feel a kind of pity—a touch of melancholy—when at this season I have wandered among withered shrubs and buried flower-beds; but here, in the wilderness, where Nature is wholly independent of art, she does not die, nor yet mourn; she lies down to rest on the bosom of Winter, and the aged one folds her in his robe of ermine and jewels, and rocks her with his hurricanes, and hushes her to sleep. How still it was! how calm, how vast the glittering white waste and the dark purple forests! The sun shone out, and the sky was without a cloud; yet we saw few people, and for many miles the hissing of our sleigh, as we flew along upon our dazzling path, and the tinkling of the sleigh-bells, were the only sounds we heard. When we were within four or five miles of the Falls, I stopped the sleigh from time to time to listen for the roar of the cataracts, but the state of the atmosphere was not favorable for the transmission of sound, and the silence was unbroken.

Such was the deep, monotonous tranquillity which prevailed on every side—so exquisitely pure and vestal-like the robe in which all nature lay slumbering around us, I could scarce believe that this whole frontier district is not only remarkable for the prevalence of vice, but of dark and desperate crime.

Mr. A., who is a magistrate, pointed out to me a lonely house by the way-side, where, on a dark stormy night in the preceding winter, he had surprised and arrested a gang of forgers and coiners; it was a fearful description. For some time my impatience had been thus beguiled—impatience and suspense much like those of a child at a theatre before the curtain rises. My imagination had been so impressed by the vast height of the Falls, that I was constantly looking in an upward direction, when, as we came to the brow of a hill, my companion suddenly checked the horses, and exclaimed, "The Falls!"

I was not, for an instant, aware of their presence; we were yet at a distance, looking *down* upon them; and I saw at once glance a flat extensive plain; the sun having withdrawn its beams for the moment, there was neither light, nor shade, nor color. In the midst were seen the two great cataracts, but merely as a feature in the wide landscape. The sound was by no means overpowering, and the clouds of spray, which Fanny Butler called so beautifully the "everlasting incense of the waters," now condensed ere they rose by the excessive cold, fell round the base of the cataracts in fleecy folds, just concealing that furious embrace of the waters above and the waters below. All the associations which in imagination I had gather round the scene, its appalling terrors, its soul-subduing beauty, power and height, and velocity and immensity, were all diminished in effect, or wholly lost.

*   *   *   *

I was quite silent—my very soul sunk within me. On seeing my disappointment (written, I suppose, most legibly in my countenance) my companion began to comfort me, by telling me of all those who had been disappointed on the first view of Niagara, and had confessed it. I *did* confess; but I was not to be comforted. We held on our way to the Clifton hotel, at the foot of the hill; most desolate it looked with its summer verandahs and open balconies cumbered up with snow, and hung round with icicles—its forlorn, empty rooms, broken windows, and dusty dinner tables. The poor people who kept the house in winter had gathered themselves for warmth and comfort into a little kitchen, and when we made our appearance, stared at us with a blank amazement, which showed what a rare thing was the sight of a visitor at this season.

While the horses were cared for, I went up into the highest balcony to command a better view of the cataracts; a little Yankee boy, with a shrewd, sharp face, and twinkling black eyes, acting as my gentleman usher. As I stood gazing on the scene which seemed to enlarge upon my vision, the little fellow stuck his hands into his pockets, and looking up in my face, said,

"You be from the old country, I reckon?"

"Yes."

"Out over there, beyond the sea?"

"Yes."

"And did you come all that way across the sea for these here Falls?"

"Yes."

"My!!" Then after a long pause, and eyeing me with a most comical expression of impudence and fun, he added, "Now, do *you* know what them 'ere birds are, out yonder?" pointing to a number of gulls which were hovering and sporting amid the spray, rising and sinking and wheeling around, appearing to delight in playing on the verges of this "hell of waters" and almost dipping their wings into the foam. My eyes were, in truth, fixed on these fair, fearless creatures, and they had suggested already twenty fanciful similitudes, when I was roused by this question.

"Those birds?" said I. "Why, *what* are they?"

"Why, them's EAGLES!"

"Eagles?" it was impossible to help laughing.

"Yes," said the urchin sturdily; "and I guess you have none of them in the old country?"

"Not many eagles, my boy; but plenty of *gulls!*" and I gave him a pretty considerable pinch by the ear.

"Ay!" said he, laughing; "well now, you be dreadful smart—smarter than many folks that come here!"

We now prepared to walk to the Crescent fall, and I bound some crampons to my feet, like those they use among the Alps, without which I could not for a moment have kept my footing on the frozen surface of the snow. As we approached the Table Rock, the whole scene assumed a wild and wonderful magnificence; down came the dark-green waters, hurrying with them over the edge of the precipice enormous blocks of ice brought down from Lake Erie. On each side of the Falls, from the ledges and overhanging cliffs, were suspended huge icicles, some twenty, some thirty feet in length, thicker than the body of a man, and in color of a paly green, like the glaciers of the Alps; and all the crags below, which projected from the boiling eddying waters, were incrusted, and in a manner built round with ice, which had formed into immense crystals, like basaltic columns, such as I have seen in the pictures of Staffa and the Giant's Causeway; and every tree, and leaf, and branch, fringing the rocks and ravines, were wrought in ice. On them, and on the wooden buildings erected near the Table Rock, the spray from the cataract had accumulated and formed into the most beautiful crystals and tracery work; they looked like houses of glass, welded and moulded into regular ornamental shapes, and hung round with a rich fringe of icy points. Wherever we stood we were on unsafe ground, for the snow, when heaped up as now to the height of three or four feet, frequently slipped in masses from the bare rock, and on its surface the spray, for ever falling, was converted into a sheet of ice, smooth, compact, and glassy, on which I could not have stood a moment without my *crampons*. It was very fearful, and yet I could not tear myself away, but remained on the Table Rock, even on the very edge of it, till a kind of dreamy fascination came over me; the continuous thunder, and might and movement of the lapsing waters, held all my vital spirits bound up as by a spell. Then, as at last I turned away, the descending sun broke out, and an Iris appeared below the American Fall, one extremity resting on a snow-mound; and motionless there it hung in the midst of restless terrors, its beautiful but rather pale hues contrasting with the death-like colorless objects around; it reminded me of the faint ethereal smile of a dying martyr.

We wandered about for nearly four hours, and then returned to the hotel: there my good-natured escort from Toronto, Mr. Campbell, was waiting to conduct us to his house, which is finely situated on an eminence not far from the great cataract. We did not know, till we arrived there, that the young and lovely wife of our host had been confined only the day before. This event had been concealed from us, lest we should have some scruples about accepting hospitality under such circumstances; and, in truth, I *did* feel at first a little uncomfortable, and rather *de trop*; but the genuine kindness of our reception soon overcame all scruples: we were made welcome, and soon felt ourselves so; and, for my own part, I have always sympathies ready for such occcasions, and shared very honestly in the grateful joy of these kind people. After dinner I went up into the room of the invalid—a little nest of warmth and comfort; and though the roar of the neighbouring cataract shook the house as with a universal tremor, it did not quite overpower the soft voice of the weak but happy mother, nor even the feeble wail of the new-born babe, as I took it in my arms with a whispered blessing, and it fell asleep in my lap. Poor little thing!—it was an awful sort of lullaby, that ceaseless thunder of the mighty waters ever at hand, yet no one but myself seemed to heed, or even to hear it; such is the force of custom, and the power of adaptation even in our most delicate organs.

To sleep at the hotel was impossible, and to intrude ourselves on the Campbells equally so. It was near midnight when we mounted our sleigh to return to the town of Niagara, and, as I remember, I did not utter a word during the whole fourteen miles. The air was still, though keen, the snow lay around, the whole earth seemed to slumber in a ghastly, calm repose; but the heavens were wide awake. There the Aurora Borealis was holding her revels, and dancing and flashing, and varying through all shapes and all hues —pale amber, rose tint, blood red—and the stars shone out with a fitful, restless brilliance; and every now and then a meteor would shoot athwart the skies, or fall to earth, and all around me was wild, and strange, and exciting—more like a fever dream than a reality.

To-day I am suffering, as might be expected, with pain and stiffness, unable to walk across the room; but the pain will pass; and on the whole I am glad I have made this excursion. The Falls did not make on my mind the impression I had anticipated, perhaps for that reason, even because I had *anticipated* it. Under different circumstances it might have been otherwise; but "it was sung to me in my cradle," as the Germans say,* that I should live to be disappointed—even in the Falls of Niagara.

Toronto, February 7.

Mr. B. gave me a seat in his sleigh, and after a rapid and very pleasant journey, during which I gained a good deal of information, we reached Toronto yesterday morning.

The road was the same as before—with one deviation however—it was found expedient to cross Burlington Bay on the ice, about seven miles over, the lake beneath being twenty, and five-and-twenty fathoms in depth. It was ten o'clock at night, and the only light was that reflected from the snow. The beaten track, from which it is not safe to deviate, was very narrow, and a man, in the worst, if not the last stage of intoxication, noisy and brutally reckless, was driving before us in a sleigh. All this, with the novelty of the situation, the tremendous cracking of the ice at every instant, gave me a sense of apprehension just sufficient to be exciting, rather than very unpleasant, though I will confess to a feeling of relief when we were once more on the solid earth.

B. is said to be a hard, active, clever, practical man. I liked him, and thought him intelligent and good-natured: we had much talk. Leaving his servant to drive, he would jump down, stand poised upon one of the runners, and, thus gliding smoothly along, we conversed.

It is a remarkable fact, with which you are probably acquainted. that when one growth of timber is cleared from the land, another of quite a different species springs up spon-

* "So war mir's in der Wiege gesungen," is a common phrase in the north of Germany to express something to which we are seemingly predestined.

taneously in its place. Thus, the oak or the beech succeeds to the pine, and the pine to the oak or maple. This is not accounted for, at least I have found no one yet who can give me a reason for it. We passed by a forest lately consumed by fire, and I asked why, in clearing the woods, they did not leave groups of the finest trees, or even single trees, here and there, to enbellish the country? But it seems that this is impossible—for the trees thus left standing, when deprived of the shelter and society to which they have been accustomed, uniformly perish—which, for mine own poor part, I thought very natural.

A Canadian settler *hates* a tree, regards it as his natural enemy, as something to be destroyed, eradicated, annihilated by all and any means. The idea of useful or ornamental is seldom associated here even with the most magnificent timber trees, such as among the Druids had been consecrated, and among the Greeks would have sheltered oracles and votive temples. The beautiful faith which assigned to every tree of the forest its guardian nymph, to every leafy grove its tutelary divinity, would find no votaries here. Alas! for the Dryads and Hamadryads of Canada!

There are two principal methods of killing trees in this country, besides the quick, unfailing destruction of the axe; the first by setting fire to them, which sometimes leaves the root uninjured to rot gradually and unseen, or be grubbed up at leisure, or, more generally, there remains a visible fragment of a charred and blackened stump, deformed and painful to look upon; the other method is slower, but even more effectual; a deep gash is cut through the bark into the stem, quite round the bole of the tree. This prevents the circulation of the vital juices, and by degrees the tree droops and dies. This is technically called *ringing* timber. Is not this like the two ways in which a woman's heart may be killed in this world of ours—by passion and by sorrow? But better far the swift fiery death than this "ringing," as they call it!

February 17.

"There is no *society* in Toronto," is what I hear repeated all around me—even by those who compose the only society we have. "But," you will say, "what could be expected in a remote town, which forty years ago was an uninhabited swamp, and twenty years ago only began to exist?" I really do not know what I expected, but I will tell you what I did *not* expect. I did not expect to find here in this new capital of a new country, with the boundless forest within half a mile of us on almost every side—concentrated as it were the worst evils of our old and most artificial social system at home, with none of its *agrémens*, and none of its advantages. Toronto is like a fourth- or fifth-rate provincial town with the pretentions of a capital city. We have here a petty colonial oligarchy, a self-constituted aristocracy, based upon nothing real, nor even upon any thing imaginary; and we have all the mutual jealousy and fear, and petty gossip, and mutual meddling and mean rivalship, which are common in a small society of which the members are well known to each other, a society composed, like all societies, of many heterogeneous particles; but as these circulate within very confined limits, there is no getting out of the way of what one most dislikes: we must necessarily hear, see, and passively endure much that annoys and disgusts any one accustomed to the independence of a large and liberal society, or the ease of continental life. It is curious enough to see how quickly a new fashion, or a new folly, is imported from the old country, and with what difficulty and delay a new idea finds its way into the heads of the people, or a new book into their hands. Yet, in the midst of all this, I cannot but see that good spirits and corrective principles are at work; that progress is making: though the march of intellect be not here in double quick time, as in Europe, it does not absolutely stand stock-still.

There reigns here a hateful factious spirit in political matters, but for the present no public or patriotic feeling, no recognition of general or generous principles of policy: as yet I have met with none of these. Canada is a colony, not a *country;* it is not yet identified with the dearest affections and associations, remembrances, and hopes of its inhabitants: it is to them an adopted, not a real mother. Their love, their pride, are not for poor Canada, but for high and happy England; but a few more generations must change all this.

We have here Tories, Whigs, and Radicals, so called; but these words do not signify exactly what we mean by the same designations at home.

You must recollect that the first settlers in Upper Canada were those who were obliged to fly from the United States during the revolutionary war, in consequence of their attachment to the British government, and the soldiers and non-commissioned officers who had fought during the war. These were recompensed for their losses, sufferings, and services, by grants of land in Upper Canada. Thus the very first elements out of which our social system was framed, were repugnance and contempt for the new institutions of the United States, and a dislike to the people of that country—a very natural result of foregoing causes; and thus it has happened that the slightest tinge of democratic, or even liberal principles in politics, was for a long time a sufficient impeachment of the loyalty, a stain upon the personal character, of those who held them. The Tories have therefore been hitherto the influential party; in their hands we find the government patronage, the principal offices, the sales and grants of land, for a long series of years.

Another party, professing the same boundless loyalty to the mother country, and the same dislike for the principles and institutions of their Yankee neighbors, may be called the Whigs of Upper Canada; these look with jealousy and scorn on the power and prejudices of the Tory families, and insist on the necessity of many reforms in the colonial government. Many of these are young men of talent, and professional men, who find themselves shut out from what they regard as their fair proportion of social consideration and influence, such as, in a small society like this, their superior education and character ought to command for them.

Another set are the Radicals, whom I generally hear mentioned as "those scoundrels," or "those rascals," or with some epithet expressive of the utmost contempt and disgust. They are those who wish to see this country erected into a republic, like the United States. A few among them are men of talent and education, but at present they are neither influential nor formidable.

There is among all parties a general tone of complaint and discontent—a mutual distrust—a langour and supineness—the causes of which I cannot as yet understand. Even those who are enthusiastically British in heart and feeling, who sincerely believe that it is the true interest of the colony to remain under the control of the mother country, are as discontented as the rest: they bitterly denounce the ignorance of the colonial officials at home, with regard to the true interests of the country: they ascribe the want of capital for improvement on a large scale to no mistrust in the resources of the country, but to a want of confidence in the measures of the government, and the security of property.

In order to understand something of the feelings which prevail here, you must bear in mind the distinction between the two provinces of Upper and Lower Canada. The project of uniting them once more into one legislature, with a central metropolis, is most violently opposed by those whose personal interests and convenience would suffer materially by a change in the seat of government. I have heard some persons go so far as to declare, that if the union of the two provinces were to be established by law, it were sufficient to absolve a man from his allegiance. On the other hand, the measure has powerful advocates in both provinces.* It seems, on looking over the map of this vast and magnificent country, and reading its whole history, that the political division into five provinces,† each with its independent governor and legislature, its separate correspondence with the Colonial-office, its local laws, and local taxation, must certainly add to the amount of colonial patronage, and perhaps render more secure the subjection of the whole to the British crown; but may it not also have perpetuated local distinctions and jealousies—kept alive divided interests, narrowed the resources, and prevented the improvement of the country on a large and general scale?

But I had better stop here, ere I get beyond my depth. I am not one of those who opine sagely, that women have nothing to do with politics. On the contrary; but I do seriously think, that no one, be it man or woman, ought to talk, much less write, on what they do not understand. Not but that I have my own ideas on these matters, though we were never able to make out, either to my own satisfaction or to yours, whether I am a Whig, or Tory, or Radical. In

* A very clever paper on this subject was published in the Quebec Mercury, Sept. 14th, 1837.

† Viz. Upper Canada, Lower Canada, Nova Scotia, New Brunswick, and Prince Edward's Island.

politics I acknowledge but two parties—those who hope and those who fear. In morals, but two parties—those who lie and those who speak truth: and all the world I divide into those who love, and those who hate. This comprehensive arrangement saves me a vast deal of trouble, and answers all my own purposes to admiration.

February 18.

Toronto is, as a residence, worse and better than other small communities—*worse* in so much as it is remote from all the best advantages of a high state of civilization, while it is infected by all its evils, all its follies; and *better*, because, besides being a small place, it is a *young* place; and in spite of this affectation of looking back, instead of looking up, it must advance—it may become the thinking head and beating heart of a nation, great, wise, and happy; who knows? And there are moments when, considered under this point of view, it assumes an interest even to me; but at present it is in a false position, like that of a youth aping maturity; or rather like that of the little boy in Hogarth's picture, dressed in a long-flapped laced waistcoat, ruffles, and cocked-hat, crying for bread and butter. With the interminable forests within half a mile of us—the haunt of the red man, the wolf, the bear—with an absolute want of the means of the most ordinary mental and moral development, we have here conventionalism in its most oppressive and ridiculous forms. If I should say, that at present the people here want cultivation, want polish, and the means of acquiring either, *that* is natural —is intelligible—and it were unreasonable to expect it could be otherwise; but if I say they want honesty, *you* would understand me, *they* would not; they would imagine that I accused them of false weights and cheating at cards. So far they are certainly "indifferent honest" after a fashion, but never did I hear so little truth, nor find so little mutual benevolence. And why is it so?—because in this place, as in other small provincial towns, they live under the principle of fear —they are afraid of each other, afraid to be themselves; and where there is much fear, there is little love, and less truth.

I was reading this morning * of Maria d'Escobar, a Spanish

* In the Life of Sir James Mackintosh.

lady, who first brought a few grains of wheat into the city of Lima. For three years she distributed the produce, giving twenty grains to one man, thirty grains to another, and so on—*hence all the corn in Peru.*

Is there no one who will bring a few grains of truth to Toronto?

February 21.

The monotony of this, my most monotonous existence, was fearfully broken last night. I had gone early to my room, and had just rung for my maid, when I was aware of a strange light flashing through the atmosphere—a fire was raging in the lower parts of the city. I looked out; there was the full moon, brighter than ever she shows her fair face in our dear cloudy England—bright and calm as you now behold her in the Mediterranean, looking down upon the snowy landscape, and the icy bay glittered like a sheet of silver; and on the other side of the heavens all was terror and tumult—clouds of smoke, mingled with spires of flame, rose into the sky. Far off the garrison was beating to arms—the bells tolling; yet all around there was not a living being to be seen, and the snow-waste was still as death.

Fires are not uncommon in Toronto, where the houses are mostly wood; they have generally an alarum once or twice a week, and six or eight houses burned in the course of the winter; but it was evident this was of more fearful extent than usual. Finding, on inquiry, that all the household had gone off to the scene of action, my own maid excepted, I prepared to follow, for it was impossible to remain here idly gazing on the flames, and listening to the distant shouts in ignorance and suspense. The fire was in the principal street (King-street), and five houses were burning together. I made my way through the snow-heaped, deserted streets, and into a kind of court or garden at the back of the blazing houses. There was a vast and motley pile of household stuff in the midst, and a poor woman keeping guard over it, nearly up to her knees in the snow. I stood on the top of a bedstead, leaning on her shoulder, and thus we remained till the whole row of buildings had fallen in. The Irishmen (God bless my countrymen! for in all good—all mischief—all frolic—all danger—they are sure to be the first) risked their lives most bravely; their dark figures moving to and fro amid the blazing rafters, their fine attitudes, and the recklessness with which they flung themselves into the most horrible situations, became at last too fearfully exciting. I was myself so near, and the flames were so tremendous, that one side of my face was scorched and blistered.

All this time, the poor woman on whose shoulder I was leaning, stood silent and motionless, gazing with apparent tranquillity on her burning house. I remember saying to her with a shudder—"But this is dreadful! to stand by and look on while one's home and property are destroyed!" And she replied quietly, "Yes, ma'am; but I dare say some good will come of it. All is for the best, if one knew it; and now Jemmy's safe, I don't care for the rest." Now Jemmy was not her son, as I found, but a poor little orphan, of whom she took charge.

There had been at first a scarcity of water but a hole being hewed through the ice on the lake, the supply was soon quick and plentiful. All would have been well over, if the sudden fall of a stack of chimneys had not caused some horrible injuries. One poor boy was killed, and some others maimed—poor Mr. B. among the number. After this I returned home rather heart-sick, and nigh to the house a sleigh glanced by at a full gallop, on which I could just perceive, in the moonlight, the extended form of a man with his hands clenched over his head—as in agony, or lifeless.

Talking this morning of the incidents of last night, several people have attempted to comfort themselves and me too with the assurance, that whatever might be the private loss or suffering, a fire was always a *public* benefit in Toronto—a good brick house was sure to arise in the place of a wooden one. It may be so—brick houses are better certainly than wooden ones—safer too; but as a general argument, I never can bear to think that any public benefit can be based on individual suffering: I hate the doctrine, and am not convinced by the logic. In these days of political economy, it is too much a fashion to consider human beings only in masses. Wondrous, and vast, and all-important as is this wide frame of human society, with all its component elements variously blended—all its magnificent destinies—is it more important in the sight of God, more fearful, more sublime to contemplate, than that mysterious world of powers, and affections, and aspirations, which we call the human soul?

In what regards government and politics, do we not find the interest of the many sacrificed to the few; while, in all that regards society, the morals and the happiness of individuals are sacrificed to the many? and both are wrong. I never can bring myself to admire a social system, in which the honor, rights, or happiness of any individual, though the meanest, is made to yield to a supposed future or general good. It is a wicked calculation, and it will be found as inexpedient as it is wicked.

February 27.

I have had a visit this morning from a man I must introduce to you more particularly. My friend, Col. F., would have pleased me any where, but here he is really invaluable.

Do you remember that lyric of Wordsworth, "The Reverie of Poor Susan," in which he describes the emotions of a poor servant-girl from the country, whose steps are arrested in Cheapside by the song of a caged bird?

> 'Tis a note of enchantment—what ails her? she sees
> A mountain ascending, a vision of trees;
> And a single small cottage, a nest like a dove's,
> The one only dwelling on earth that she loves!
>
> She looks, and her heart is in heaven!

And how near are human hearts allied in all natural instincts and sympathies, and what an unfailing, universal fount of poetry are these even in their homeliest forms! F. told me to-day, that once, as he was turning down a bye street in this little town, he heard somewhere near him the song of the lark. (Now, you must observe, there are no larks in Canada but those which are brought from the old country.) F. shall speak in his own words: "So, ma'am, when I heard the voice of the bird in the air, I looked, by the natural instinct, up to the heavens, though I knew it could not be there, and then on this side, and then on that, and sure enough at last I saw the little creature perched on its sod of turf in a little cage, and there it kept trilling and warbling away, and there I stood stock-still—listening with my heart. Well, I don't know what it was at all that came over me, but every thing seemed to change before my eyes, and it was in poor Ireland I was again, and my home all about me, and I was again a wild slip of a boy, lying on my back on the hill-side above my mother's cabin, and watching, as I used to do, the lark singing and soaring over my head, and I straining my eye to follow her till she melted into the blue sky—and there, ma'am—would you believe it?—I stood like an old fool listening to the bird's song, lost, as in a dream, and there I think I could have stood till this day." And the eyes of the rough soldier filled with tears, even while he laughed at himself, as perfectly unconscious that he was talking poetry, as Mons. Jourdain could be that he was talking prose.

Colonel F. is a soldier of fortune—which phrase means, in *his* case at least, that he owes nothing whatever to fortune, but every thing to his own good heart, his own good sense, and his own good sword. He was the son, and glories in it, of an Irish cotter, on the estate of the Knight of Glyn. At the age of fifteen he shouldered a musket, and joined a regiment which was ordered to Holland at the time the Duke of York was opposed to Dumourier. His only reading up to this time had been "The Seven Champions of Christendom," and "The Seven Wise Masters." With his head full of these examples of chivarly, he marched to his first battle-field, vowing to himself, that if there were a dragon to be fought, or a giant to be defied, he would be their man!—at all events, he would enact some valorous exploit, some doughty deed of arms, which should astonish the world and dub him captain on the spot. He then described with great humor and feeling his utter astonishment and mortification on finding the mechanical slaughter of a modern field of battle so widely different from the picture of his fancy;—when he found himself one of a mass in which the individual heart and arm, however generous, however strong, went for nothing—forced to stand still, to fire only by the word of command—the chill it sent to his heart, and his emotions when he saw the comrade at his side fall a quivering corpse at his feet—all this he described with a graphic liveliness and simplicity which was very amusing. He was afterwards taken prisoner, and at the time he was so overcome by the idea of the indignity he had incurred by being captured and stripped, and of the affliction and dishonor that would fall on his mother, that he was tempted to commit suicide in the old Roman fashion; but on seeing a lieutenant of his own regiment brought in prisoner, he thought better of it; a dishonor which the lieutenant endured with philosophy, might, he thought, be borne by a subaltern, for by this time, at the age of eighteen, he was already sergeant.

He was soon afterwards exchanged, and ordered out to Canada with his regiment, the Forty-ninth. He obtained his commission as lieutenant in the same regiment by mere dint of bravery and talent; but as his pay was not sufficient to enable him to live like his brother officers and purchase his accoutrements, the promotion he had earned by his good conduct became, for a long time, a source of embarrassment. During the last American war he performed a most brilliant exploit, for which he received his captain's commission on the field. Immediately after receiving it, he astonished his commander by asking leave of absence, although another battle was expected in a few days. The request was, in truth, so extraordinary that General Sheaffe hesitated, and at last refused. F. said, that if his request was granted, he would be again at headquarters within three days; if refused, he would go without leave. "For," said he, "I was desperate, and the truth was, ma'am, there was a little girl that I loved, and I knew that if I could but marry her before I was killed, and I a captain, she would have the pension of a captain's widow. It was all I could leave her, and it would have been some comfort to me, though not to her, poor soul!"

Leave of absence was granted; F. mounted his horse, rode a hundred and fifty miles in an exceedingly short time, married his little girl, and returned the day following to his duties, and to fight another battle, in which, however, he was not killed, but has lived to be the father of a fine family of four brave sons and one gentle daughter.

The men who have most interested me through life were all self-educated, and what are called originals. This dear, good F. is *originalissimo*. Some time ago he amused me, and gave me at the same time a most vivid idea of the minor horrors and irremediable mischiefs of war, by a description of his being quartered in a church in Flanders. The soldiers, on taking possession of their lodging, began by breaking open the poor-boxes and ransacking the sacristie. They then broke up the chairs and benches for fires to cook their rations, and these not sufficing, the wooden saints and carved altars were soon torn down. Finding themselves incommoded by the smoke, some of the soldiers climbed up by the projecting ornaments and smashed through the windows of rich stained glass to admit the air and let out the smoke. The next morning at sunrise they left this sanctuary of religion and art a foul defaced ruin. A century could not make good again the pollution and spoliation of those few hours.

"You must not be too hard on us poor soldiers," added F., as if answering to a look, for I did not comment aloud. "I had a sort of instinctive perception of the mischief we were doing, but I was certainly the only one; they knew no better, and the precarious life of a soldier gives him the habit of sacrificing every thing to the present moment and a certain callousness to the suffering and destruction which, besides that it ministers to the immediate want, is out of sight and forgotten the next instant. Why I was not quite so insensible as the rest, I cannot tell, unless it was through the goodness of God. When I was a boy, my first feeling, *next to my love for my mother*, was gratitude to God for having made me and called me into being out of nothing. My first thought was what I could do to please him. Now, in spite of all the priest might say, I could not perceive that fasting and praying would do *Him* any good, so I looked about in the fulness of my heart to see what I *could* do—and I fancied there was a voice which whispered continually, 'Do good to your neighbor, do good to your neighbor!' "

With so much overflowing benevolence and fearless energy of character, and all the eccentricity, and sensibility, and poetry, and headlong courage of his country, you cannot wonder that this brave and worthy man interests me; unluckily, I can see him seldom, his life being one of almost unremitting toil.

March 1.

In the different branches of art, each artist thinks his own the highest, and is filled with the idea of all its value and all its capabilities which he understands best and has most largely studied and developed. "But," says Dr. Chalmers, "we must take the testimony of each man to the worth of that which he does know, and reject the testimony of each to the comparative worthlessness of that which he does not know."

For it is not, generally speaking, that he overrates his own particular walk of art from over-enthusiasm (no art, when considered separately, as a means of human delight and improvement, *can* be overrated), but such a *one-sided* artist underrates from ignorance the walks of others which diverge from his own.

Of all artists, musicians are most exclusive in devotion to their own art, and in the want of sympathy, if not absolute contempt, for other arts. A painter has more sympathies with a musician, than a musician with a painter. Vernet used to bring his easel into Pergolesi's room, to paint beside his harpsicord, and used to say that he owed some of his finest skies to the inspired harmonies of his friend. Pergolesi never felt, perhaps, any harmonies but those of his own delicious art.

"Aspasia, he who loves not music is a beast of one species, and he who overloves it, is a beast of another, whose brain is smaller than a nightingale's, and his heart than that of a lizard!" I refer you for the rest to a striking passage in Landor's "Pericles and Aspasia," containing a most severe philippic, not only against the professors, but the *profession* of music, and which concludes very aptly, "Panenus said this: let us never believe a word of it!" It is too true that some excellent musicians have been ignorant, and sensual, and dissipated, but there are sufficient exceptions to the sweeping censure of Panenus to show that "imprudence, intemperance, and gluttony," do not always, or necessarily, "open their channels into the sacred stream of music." Musicians are not selfish, careless, sensual, ignorant, because they are musicians, but because, from a defective education, they are nothing else. The German musicians are generally more moral and more intellectual men than English or Italian musicians, and hence their music has taken a higher flight, is more intellectual than the music of other countries. Music as an art has not degraded them, but they have elevated music.

It is impeaching the goodness of the beneficent Creator to deem that moral evil can be inseparably connected with any of the fine arts—least of all with music—the soul of the physical, as love is of the moral, universe.

The most accomplished and intellectual musician I ever met with is Felix Mendelsohn. I do not recollect if it were himself or some one else who told me of a letter which Carl von Weber had addressed to him, warning him that he never could attain the highest honors in his profession without cultivating the virtues and the decencies of life. "A great artist," said Weber, "ought to be a good man."

While I am "i' the vein," I must give you a few more musical reminiscences before my fingers are quite frozen.

I had once some conversation with Thalberg and Felix Mendelsohn, on the unmeaning names which musicians often give to their works, as Concerto in F, Concerto in B b, First Symphony, Second Symphony, &c. Mendelsohn said, that although in almost every case the composer might have a leading idea, it would be often difficult, or even impossible, to give any title sufficiently comprehensive to convey the same idea or feeling to the mind of the hearer.

But music, except to musicians, can only give ideas, or rather raise images, by association; it can give the pleasure which the just accordance of musical sounds must give to sensitive ears, but the associated ideas or images, if any, must be quite accidental. Haydn, we are told, when he sat down to compose, used first to invent a story in his own fancy—a regular succession of imaginary incidents and feelings—to which he framed or suited the successive movements (motivi) of his concerto. Would it not have been an advantage if Haydn could have given to his composition such a title as would have pitched the imagination of the listener at once upon the same key? Mendelsohn himself has done this in the pieces which he has entitled "Overture to Melusina," "Overture to the Hebrides," "Meeres Stille und Glückliche Fahrt," "The Brook," and others—which is better surely than Sonata No. 1, Sonata No. 2. Take the Melusina, for example; Is there not in the sentiment of the music, all the sentiment of the beautiful old fairy tale?—first, in the flowing, intermingling harmony, we have the soft elemental delicacy of the water nymph; then, the gushing of fountains, the undulating waves; then the martial prowess of the knightly lover, and the splendor of chivalry prevailing over the softer and more ethereal nature; and then, at last, the dissolution of the charm; the ebbing, fainting, and failing away into silence of the beautiful water spirit. You will say it might answer just as well for Ondine; but this signifies little, provided we have our fancy pitched to certain poetical associations pre-existing in the composer's mind. Thus, not only poems, but pictures and statues, might be set to music. I suggested to Thalberg as a subject the Aurora of Guido. It should begin with a slow, subdued, and solemn movement, to express the slumbrous softness of that dewy hour which precedes the coming of the day, and which in the picture broods over the distant landscape, still wrapt in darkness and sleep; then the stealing upwards of the gradual dawn; the brightening, the quickening of all life; the awakening of the birds, the burst of the sunlight, the rushing of the steeds of Hyperion through the sky, the aerial dance of the Hours, and the whole concluding with a magnificent choral song of triumph and rejoicing sent up from universal nature.

And then in the same spirit—no, in his own grander spirit —I would have Mendelsohn improviser the Loacoon. There would be the pomp and procession of the sacrifice on the sea-shore; the flowing in of the waves; the two serpents which come gliding on their foamy crests, wreathing, and rearing, and undulating; the horror, the lamentation, the clash of confusion, the death struggle, and, after a deep pause, the wail of lamentation, the funereal march; the whole closing with a hymn to Apollo. Can you not just imagine such a piece of music, and composed by Mendelsohn? and can you not fancy the possibility of setting to music in the same manner, Raffaelle's Cupi and Psyche, or his Galatea, or the group of the Niobe? Niobe would be a magnificent subject either for a concerto, or for a kind of mythological oratorio.

❦

March 2.

Turning over to Boswell to-day, I came upon this passage: Johnson says, "I do not commend a society where there is an agreement that what would not otherwise be fair shall be fair; but I maintain that an individual of any society who practises what is allowed, is not dishonest."

What say you to this reasoning of our great moralist? Does it not reduce the whole moral law to something merely conventional?

In another place, Dr. Johnson asks, "What proportion does climate bear to the complex system of human life?" I shiver while I answer, "A good deal, my dear Doctor, to some individuals, and yet more to whole races of men."

He says afterwards, "I deal more in *notions* than in facts." And so do I, it seems.

He talks of "men being *held down* in conversation by the presence of women"—*held up*, rather, where moral feeling is concerned; and if held down where intellect and social interests are concerned, then so much the worse for such a state of society.

Johnson knew absolutely nothing about women; witness that one assertion, among others more insulting, that it is matter of indifference to a woman whether her husband be faithful or not. He says, in another place, "If we men require more perfection from women than from ourselves, it is doing them honor."

Indeed! If, in exacting from us more perfection, you do not allow us the higher and nobler nature, you do us not honor but gross injustice; and if you do allow us the higher nature, and yet regard us as subject and inferior, then the injustice is the greater. There, Doctor, is a dilemma for you.

Of all our modern authors, Coleridge best understood the essential nature of women, and has said the truest and most beautiful things of our sex generally; and of all our modern authors, Hazlitt was most remarkable for his utter ignorance of women, generally and individually.

Charles Lamb, of all the men I ever talked to, had the most kindly, the most compassionate, the most reverential feelings towards women; but he did not, like Coleridge, set forth these feelings with elaborate eloquence—they came gushing out of his heart and stammering from his tongue—clothed sometimes in the quaintest disguise of ironical abuse, and sometimes in words which made the tears spring to one's eyes. He seemed to understand us not as a poet, nor yet as a man of the world; but by the unerring instinct of the most loving and benevolent of hearts.

When Coleridge said antithetically, "that it was the beauty of a woman's character to be characterless," I suppose it is as if he had said, "It is the beauty of the diamond to be colorless;" for he instances Ophelia and Desdemona; and though they are colorless in their pure, transparent simplicity, they are as far as possible from characterless, for in the very quality of being colorless consists the character.

Speaking of Coleridge reminds me that it was from Ludwig Tieck I first learned the death of this wonderful man;

and as I, too, had "sat at the feet of Gamaliel and heard his words," the news struck me with a solemn sorrow. I remember that Tieck, in announcing the death of Coleridge, said, in his impressive manner, "A great spirit has passed from the world, and the world knew him not."

There are two ladies in Toronto who have conservatories, a proof of advancing wealth, and civilization, and taste, which you will greatly admire. One of them had the kindness to send me a bouquet of hot-house flowers while I was ill this last time; and a gift of fifty times the value could not have excited the same pleasure and gratitude. I spread the flowers out on my bed, and inhaled their fragrance with emotions I dare hardly confess—even to you. I had not seen a flower since I left England.

Yesterday (March 4th) our provincial parliament was prorogued by the governor in state, and I had the honour of *assisting*, as the French say, on that important occasion.

Now you would not ask me, nor do I feel inclined, to encumber my little note-book (consecrated to far different purposes, far different themes) with information to be obtained in every book of travels and statistics; but it is just possible that you *may* know as little of our political constitution and forms of proceeding as I did before my arrival in Upper Canada, and I wish to make the scene of yesterday as intelligible and as interesting to you as I can, so I will give you, in as few words as possible, a sketch of our state machinery.

I have mentioned to you (I believe) that the division of the province of Quebec into Upper and Lower Canada took place in 1791; at that time a chartered constitution and a separate executive and legislative government were conferred on each province: a measure well intended, doubtless, but of which the wisdom was more than doubtful, when we consider the results.

Our constitution of Upper Canada seems, at first view, that of the mother country in miniature, and identical with it. For instance, we have, as the head of our executive, a governor, subject, in his military capacity, to the governor-in-chief of Lower Canada, but in all other respects dependent only on the government at home, assisted by an executive council appointed by himself; and we have a legislature composed of a legislative council, nominated by the government, and a house of assembly delegated by the people. These different branches seem to represent, not unfitly, the sovereign, the cabinet of ministers, the House of Lords, and the House of Commons, in England.

But there are some important distinctions which tend to secure the dependence of the provincial legislature on the executive government at home; for I do not know that our parliament has hitherto *legislated* for the colonies.

When Sir Francis Head arrived here the executive council consisted of five; he added three to the number, who were noted Reformers. About three weeks afterwards this executive council addressed to the governor a document, in which they assumed as their right precisely the same powers and responsibilities as those of the cabinet ministers at home, alleging, that although nominated by the governor, they hold themselves responsible to the will of the people.

To which document Sir Francis replied to this effect—"that though the constitution of the colony resembled, it was not to be considered as identical with, the constitution of the mother country:—that if the lieutenant-governor stood in place of the sovereign—if, like the sovereign, he could *do no wrong*, then it would be evident that a ministry, an executive council, or some other body of men, should be appointed, who might be responsible to the country for their conduct. But this was not the case. The lieutenant-governor was delegated by the king, not as the representative, but as the responsible minister of the sovereign, subject to impeachment for neglecting the interests of the people, and liable to immediate recall; and that, under such circumstances, to render the lieutenant-governor responsible for the acts of an executive council, which was responsible only to the people, was a manifest injustice, as well as an anomaly."

All which seems to me a very clear case as thus stated. The governor also denied not only any right or power of his own to alter one letter or iota of the constitution, but all power in the united legislature of Upper Canada to alter or *improve* the political constitution of the country, as by law established, this power resting only with the executive in England. From all which it appears, as far as I can understand, that the government of this province is not derived from the people who inhabit it, nor responsible to them nor their delegates.

Immediately on receiving this answer, the six councillors who had presented the document or remonstrance above-mentioned, resigned their seats in the council, and Sir Francis immediately appointed four others. The president of the executive council—that is, the *Premier* of our cabinet of ministers—is Mr. Sullivan.

The legislative council varies in number: at present there are, I believe, thirty members. Of these, twenty-one are Scotch and Canadians, and nine English, Irish, and Americans. They represent the aristocracy of the country, but differ from the House of Lords, in not being hereditary; they are nominated for life by the governor. The speaker is the Chief Justice Robinson, a Tory in politics, and a very able and accomplished man.

The House of Assembly consists of the delegates of the people, the number increasing with the population. As soon as the number of inhabitants in a town or country amounts to a certain number fixed by law, they have the right of choosing one or two representatives in parliament. The House of Assembly consisted, in 1831, of about forty members. At present there are twenty-two counties which send each two members to parliament; three counties which send only one member; and the four ridings of York, and the four ridings of Lincoln, each one member; and seven towns each one member: in all sixty-two members. Of these, forty-four are Conservative members, and eighteen are Reformers. In the former House of Assembly, dissolved by Sir Francis Head in 1836, the majority were Radicals, or opposed to the British supremacy. The best speakers on the Conservative side are, Hagerman, the Solicitor-general,* a Tory in politics, a man of great ability and good nature, but somewhat coarse and overbearing in character and manner; Draper, the member for Toronto,† a clever active-minded man, and a fluent speaker; M'Nab,‡ the member for Wentworth, also an able and influential man of large property; and Mr. Prince, member for Sandwich, a gentleman educated at the English bar, and of very superior attainments, liberal, though not revo-

* Now Attorney-general.
† Now Solicitor-general.
‡ Afterwards Speaker of the House of Assembly.

lutionary, in principle. On the opposition side, the cleverest man and most eloquent speaker is Dr. Rolph.

The members are paid for their attendance during the session at the rate of ten shillings a day.

This slight sketch will give you some general idea of the political constitution and the state of parties in Upper Canada.

The prorogation took place yesterday at three o'clock; when we arrived in front of the government offices the scene was very striking. The snow-expanse was all around, and between the shore of the frozen bay and the line of building, the space was filled by sleighs of all shapes and sizes, the horses curveting and kicking up the snow, and a crowd of some hundred people in all manner of strange defences against the piercing frost, intermingled with military costumes, and a few Indians lounging by in their blanket-coats and war-plumes.

The hall of the legislative council is a subject of great pride to the Canadians. It is certainly a spacious and lofty room, with a splendid throne and the usual superfluity of gilding and varnish; yet the interior decorations (the admiration of the people here) are in the vilest possible taste—which critical observation I make in no offensive spirit; any thing which is *attempted* here, beyond the putting together of a log-house, is praiseworthy. We must have time—time! "E coll' Tempo, tutto!" On the right of the throne sat Chief Justice Robinson; he has a fine head and acute features, and the most pleasing, insinuating voice I ever heard. The judges and law officers of the crown sat at a table in front, and the other members of the legislative council were ranged on each side. My proper place was on the right, among the wives of the officials, the aristocracy of Toronto. The toilettes around me were gay and pretty, in the fashion of two or three years ago, and all the ladies showed a disposition to be polite and amiable; but I was too much a stranger to join in the conversation, and there were none near me to give me any necessary explanation, or to point out any remarkable or distinguished persons, if there were such. Among the spectators opposite I remarked a man with a very extraordinary head and countenance, and I was told that he was a disciple of Edward Irving, and a preacher of the "Unknown

Tongues," and that several persons in Toronto, even members of the council, were converts to these wild doctrines.

The governor, as he alighted, was enthusiastically cheered by the populace—a circumstance rather unusual of late, and which caused a good deal of excitement and exultation around me. In a moment afterwards he entered and took his seat on the throne.

As an official representative, Sir Francis has not the advantage of the height, fine person, and military bearing of Sir John Colborne. He is a little man, with a neat, active figure, a small but intelligent head, grave and rather acute features; his bright blue eye is shrewd and quick, with an expression of mingled humor and benevolence, and his whole deportment in the highest degree unaffected and pleasing.

March 8.

Before the languid heart gasp and flutter itself to death, like a bird in an exhausted receiver, let us see what can be done, for something must be done.

This relentless winter seems to stiffen and contract every nerve, and the frost is of that fierceness and intensity, that it penetrates even to the marow of one's bones. One of the workmen told me yesterday, that on taking hold of an iron bar it had taken the skin off his hand, as if he had grasped it red hot: it is a favorite trick with the children to persuade each other to touch with the tongue a piece of metal which has been exposed to the open air; adhesion takes place immediately: even the metal knobs on the doors of the room I carefully avoid touching—the contact is worse than unpleasant.

Let but the spring come again, and I will take to myself wings and fly off to the west! But will spring *ever* come? When I look out upon the bleak, shrouded, changeless scene, there is something so awfully silent, fixed, and immutable in its aspect, that it is enough to disturb one's faith in the everlasting revolutions of the seasons. Green leaves and flowers, and streams that murmur as they flow, soft summer airs, to which we open the panting bosom—panting with too much life—shades grateful for their coolness—can such things be, or do they exist only in poetry and Paradise?

If it were not for this journalizing, I should fall into a lethargy—as it is I could envy a marmot or a dormouse; and if it were not for my promise to you, I should even abandon this daily noting of daily nothings, of which I begin to be thoroughly ashamed. One day is only distinguishable from another by the degrees of the thermometer. Nor can I, while imprisoned by this relentless climate, seek the companionship and sympathy which stand aloof—for no other reason that I can guess—but because I come among them branded with notoriety. I wished to throw open my house in the evening, and break or thaw the social frost around me; but such a novel and unheard of idea would startle all the inhabitants from their propriety. There must be here, as elsewhere, kind-hearted, good people, if only they would be natural, and not afraid of each other—and of poor, solitary me. However, in the strait in which I am placed there is still a remedy.

> "Books, dreams, are each a world; and the books we know
> Are a substantial world."

A world ever at hand. I must try all mechanical means to maintain the balance of my mind, and the unimpaired use of my faculties, for they will be needed. There is no rescue but in occupation; serious and useful occupation if I can make or find it—trivial occupation when I can *not*. The desultory reading in which I have lately indulged will never do; I must look round for something to try my strength—and force and fix my atention. To use my Lord Byron's phrase, I must get "a file for the serpent."

March 10.

I have found a *file*, or what I will use as such. I shall take to translating.

I brought from Weimar Dr. Ekermann's book,* which, as yet, I have only glanced over in parts; by this time it must be well known all over the world of literature. When I left Weimar it was not yet published. There, my attention was strongly directed to this book, not so much by the interest, as by the *kind* of interest it had excited around me. I re-

* Gespräche mit Goëthe. (Conversations with Goëthe.)

member one of Goëthe's grandsons, turning over the leaves as it lay on my table, and exclaiming with animation—"Es ist der Grosspapa selbst! da lebt er!—da spricht er!" (It is grand-papa himself!—here he lives—he speaks!")

Another, habitually intimate with the domestic life of Goëthe, said, with emotion—"Es ist das Buch von Liebe und Wahrheit." (It is the book of love and truth.)

"Whatever may be in that book," said a dear friend of mine, when she placed it in my hands, "I would pledge myself beforehand for its truth. The mind of Eckermann, at once unsullied and unruffled by all contact with the world, is so constituted, that he could not perceive or speak other than the truth, any more than a perfectly clear and smooth mirror could reflect a false or a distorted image."

Now all this was delightful! The sort of praise one does not often hear either of a book or a writer—and so, to read I do most seriously incline.

I read the preface to-day, and part of the introduction.

March 28.

About a week ago we removed into a new house, and I have since been too much occupied to go on with my studies, domestic matters having "possessed me wholly." Our present residence has never yet been inhabited, and is not quite finished. It will be very pretty and pleasant, no doubt, when it is not so *very* cold and comfortless. We are surrounded by a garden of some extent—or, rather, what will be a garden at some future time; at present it is a bleak waste of snow; we are so completely blockaded by ice and mud, that to reach the house-door is a matter of some difficulty and even danger. Planks laid from one snow heap to another form the only access to the house-door. The site, though now so dreary, must be charming in summer, for we command, at once glance, the entrance to the bay, the King's Pier, the lighthouse, and beyond, the whole expanse of Lake Ontario to the Niagara shore, which in some particular states of the atmosphere is distinctly visible, though distant nearly thirty miles. They say, that in clear summer mornings, the cloud of spray rising from the Falls can be seen from this point. There is yet no indication as the approach of spring, and I find it more than ever difficult to keep myself warm. Nothing in myself or around me feels or looks like *home*. How much is comprised in that little word! May it please God to preserve to me all that I love! But, O absence! how much is comprised in *that* word too! it is death of the heart and darkness of the soul; it is the ever-springing, ever-dying hope; the ever-craving, never-having wish; it is fear, and doubt, and sorrow, and pain;—a state in which the past swallows up the present, and the future becomes the past before it arrives!

* * * *

It is now seven weeks since the date of the last letters from my far-distant home. The archdeacon told me, by way of comfort, that when he came to settle in this country, there was only one mail-post from England in the course of a whole year, and it was called, as if in mockery, "The Express;" now, either by way of New-York or Halifax, we have a post almost every day.

April 1.

So, there is another month gone; and the snows are just beginning to disappear, and the flocks of snow-birds with them; and the ice is breaking up at the entrance of the bay, and one or two little vessels have ventured as far as the King's Wharf; and the wind blows strong to dry up the melting snow, and some time or other, perhaps, spring will come, and this long winter's imprisonment will be at an end. Yes; I have been spoiled during these last years—I have been existing only for, and by, the highest faculties of my being—have lived through admiration, hope, and love, "until aversion and contempt were things I only knew by name;" and now another time is come—how ill, how very ill I bear it!

This is the worst season in Canada. The roads are breaking up, and nearly impassable; lands are flooded, and in low situations there is much sickness, particularly ague. We have still sixteen square miles of ice within the bay.

The market at Toronto is not well supplied, and is at a great distance from us. The higher class of people are supplied with provisions from their own lands and farms, or by certain persons they know and employ. With a little management and forethought, we now get on very well; but at first we had to suffer great inconvenience. Quantities of salted provisions are still imported into the country for the consumption of the soldiers and distant settlers, and at certain seasons—at present, for example—there is some difficulty in procuring any thing else.

Our table, however, is pretty well supplied. Beef is tolerable, but lean; mutton bad, scarce, and dearer than beef; pork excellent and delicate, being fattened principally on Indian corn. The fish is of many various kinds, and delicious. During the whole winter we had black-bass and white-fish, caught in holes in the ice, and brought down by the Indians. Venison, game, and wild fowl are always to be had; the quails, which are caught in immense numbers near Toronto, are most delicate eating; I lived on them when I could eat nothing else. What they call partridge here is a small species of pheasant, also very good; and now we are promised snipes and woodcocks in abundance. The wild goose is also excellent eating when well cooked, but the old proverb about Heaven sending meat, &c. &c. is verified here. Those who have farms near the city, or a country establishment of their own, raise poultry and vegetables for their own table. As yet I have seen no vegetables whatever but potatoes; even in the best seasons they are not readily to be procured in the market. Every year, however, as Toronto increases in population and importance, will diminish these minor inconveniences.

The want of good servants is a more serious evil. I could amuse you with an account of the petty miseries we have been enduring from this cause, the strange characters who come to offer themselves, and the wages required. Almost all the servants are of the lower class of Irish emigrants, in general honest, warm-hearted, and willing; but never having seen any thing but want, dirt, and reckless misery at home, they are not the most eligible persons to trust with the cleanliness and comfort of one's household. Yet we make as many complaints, and express as much surprise at their deficiencies, as though it were possible it could be otherwise. We give to our man-servant eight dollars a month, to the cook six dollars, and to the housemaid four; but these are lower wages than are usual for good and experienced servants, who might indeed command almost any wages here, where all labor is high priced.

A carriage of some kind is here one of the necessaries of life, but a light English-built carriage would be quite unfit for the country—absolutely useless. There is, however, an excellent coachmaker here, who has turned out some very pretty equipages—both sleighs and barouches—of the build which is calculated for the roads in the neighborhood.

There are other good shops in the town, and one, that of the apothecary, worthy of Regent-street in its appearance. The importations of china, glass, hardware, and clothing, arrive from England in the spring and autumn, the seasons for making our purchases. All these articles are much dearer than in England, and there is little choice as to taste or fashion. Two years ago we bought our books at the same shop where we bought our shoes, our spades, our sugar, and salt pork; now we have two good booksellers' shops, and at one of these a circulating library of two or three hundred volumes of common novels. As soon as there is a demand for something better, there will be a supply of course; but, as I said before, we must have *time*. Archdeacon Strahan and Chief Justice Robinson have very pretty libraries, but in general it is about two years before a new work of any importance finds it way here; the American reprints of the English reviews and magazines, and the Albion newspaper, seem to supply amply our literary wants.

Apropos to newspapers—my table is covered with them. In the absence or scarcity of books, they are the principal medium of knowledge and communication in Upper Canada. There is no stamp-act here—no duty on paper; and I have sometimes thought that the great number of local newspapers which do not circulate beyond their own little town or district, must, from the vulgar, narrow tone of many of them, do mischief; but on the whole, perhaps, they do more good. Paragraphs printed from English or American papers, on subjects of general interest, the summary of political events, extracts from books or magazines, are copied from one paper into another, till they have travelled round the country. It is true that a great deal of base, vulgar, inflammatory party feeling is also circulated by the same means; but, on the whole, I should not like to see the number or circulation of the district papers checked. There are about forty published in Upper Canada; of these, three are religious, viz. the "Christian Guardian," "The Wesleyan Advocate," and "The Church;" a paper in the German language is published at Berlin, in the Gore district, for the use of the German settlers; "The Correspondent and Advocate" is the leading radical, "The Toronto Patriot," the leading Conservative paper. The newspapers of Lower Canada and the United States are circulated in great numbers; and as they pay postage, it is no inconsiderable item in the revenue of the post-office. In some of these provincial papers I have seen articles written with considerable talent; amongst other things, I have remarked a series of letters signed Evans, addressed to the Canadians on the subject of an education fitted for an agricultural people, and written with infinite good sense and kindly feeling; these have been copied from one paper into another, and circulated widely; no doubt they will do good. Last year the number of newspapers circulated through the post-office, and paying postage, was

Provincial papers . . .	178,065
United States and foreign papers .	149,502

Add 100,000 papers stamped or free, here are 427,567 papers circulated yearly among a population of 370,000, of whom, perhaps, one in fifty can read;—this is pretty well. The gross receipts of the post-office are 21,000*l*. a year. It is rather affecting to see the long lists of unclaimed letters lying at the post-office, and read the advertisements in the Canada and American journals for husbands, relatives, friends, lost or strayed.

There is a commercial news-room in the city of Toronto, and this is absolutely the only place of assembly or amusement, except the taverns and low drinking-houses. An attempt has been made to found a mechanics' institute and a literary club; but as yet they create little interest, and are very ill supported.

If the sympathy for literature and science be small, that for music is less. Owing to the exertions of an intelligent musician here, some voices have been so far drilled that the psalms and anthems at church are very tolerably performed; but this gentleman receives so little general encouragement, that he is at this moment preparing to go over to the United States. The archdeacon is collecting subscriptions to pay for an organ which is to cost a thousand pounds; if the money were expended in aid of a singing-school, it would do more good.

The interior of the episcopal church here is rather elegant, with the exception of a huge window of painted glass which cost 500*l.*, and is in a vile, tawdry taste.

Besides the episcopal church, the Presbyterians, Methodists, Roman Catholics, and Baptists have each a place of worship. There is also an African church for the negroes.

The hospital, a large brick building, is yet too small for the increasing size of the city. The public grammar-school, called the "Upper Canada College," forms a cluster of ugly brick buildings; and although the system of education there appears narrow and defective, yet it is a *beginning*, and certainly productive of good.

The physician I have mentioned to you, Dr. Rees, entertains the idea of founding a house of reception for destitute female emigrants on their arrival in Canada—a house, where, without depending on *charity*, they may be boarded and lodged at the smallest possible cost, and respectably protected till they can procure employment. You may easily imagine that I take a deep interest in this design.

There you have the result of a walk I took this morning up and down our city with a very intelligent guide.

I am afraid these trifling facts will not much interest you. For me, no facts, merely as facts, are in the slightest degree interesting, except as they lead to some truth. I must combine them, and in the combination seek or find a result, before such facts excite either my curiosity or attention.

April 15.

The ice in the bay of Toronto has been, during the winter months, from four to five feet in thickness: within the last few days it has been cracking in every direction with strange noises, and last night, during a tremendous gale from the east, it was rent, and loosened, and driven at once out of the bay. "It moveth altogether, if it move at all." The last time I drove across the bay, the ice beneath me appeared as fixed and firm as the foundations of the earth, and within twelve hours it has disappeared.

To-day the first steam-boat of the season entered our harbor. They called me to the window to see it, as, with flags and streamers flying, and amid the cheers of the people, it swept majestically into the bay. I sympathized with the general rejoicing, for I can fully understand all the animation and bustle which the opening of the navigation will bring to our torpid capital.

In former times, when people travelled into strange countries, they travelled *de bonne foi*, really to see and learn what was new to them. Now, when a traveller goes to a foreign country, it is always with a set of preconceived notions concerning it, to which he fits all he sees, and refers all he hears; and this, I suppose, is the reason that the old travellers are still safe guides; while modern travellers may be pleasant reading, but are withal the most unsafe guides any one can have.

June 13.

IN these latter days I have lived in friendly communion with so many excellent people, that my departure from Toronto was not what I anticipated—an escape on one side, or a riddance on the other. My projected tour to the west excited not only some interest, but much kind solicitude; and aid and counsel were tendered with a feeling which touched me deeply. The chief justice, in particular, sent me a whole sheet of instructions, and several letters of introduction to settlers along my line of route, Fitzgibbon, always benevolent, gave me sensible and cheerful encouragement as we walked leisurely down to the pier, to embark in the steam-boat which was to carry me across the lake to Niagara.

And here I might moralize on the good effects of being *too* early instead of too late on a journey: on the present occasion, having a quarter of an hour or twenty minutes to spare proved the most important and most fortunate circumstance which could have occurred at my outset.

The first bell of the steam-boat had not yet rung, when my good friend Dr. Rees came running up to tell me that the missionary from the Sault St. Marie, and his Indian wife, had arrived at Toronto, and were then at the inn, and that there was just time to introduce me to them. No sooner thought than done: in another moment we were in the hotel, and I was introduced to Mrs. MacMurray, otherwise O-ge-ne-bu-go-quay, (i.e. *the wild rose*).

I must confess that the specimens of Indian squaws and half-cast women I had met with, had in no wise prepared me for what I found in Mrs. MacMurray. The first glance, the first sound of her voice, struck me with a pleased surprise. Her figure is tall—at least it is rather above than below the middle size, with that indescribable grace and undulation of movement which speaks the perfection of form. Her features are distinctly Indian, but softened and refined, and their expression at once bright and kindly. Her dark eyes have a sort of fawn-like shyness in their glance, but her manner, though timid, was quite free from embarrassment or restraint. She speaks English well, with a slightly foreign intonation, not the less pleasing to my ear that it reminded me of the voice and accent of some of my German friends. In two minutes I was seated by her—my hand kindly folded in hers—and we were talking over the possibility of my plans. It seems there is some chance of my reaching the Island of Michillimackinac, but of the Sault St. Marie, I dare hardly think as yet—it looms in my imagination dimly described in far space, a kind of Ultima Thule; yet the sight of Mrs. MacMurray seemed to give something definite to the vague hope which had been floating in my mind. Her sister, she said, was married to the Indian agent at Michillimackinac,* a man celebrated in the United States for his scientific researches; and from both she promised me a welcome, should I reach their island. To her own far-off home at the Sault St. Marie, between Lake Huron and Lake Superior, she warmly invited me—without, however, being able to point out any conveyance or mode of travel thither that could be depended on—only a possible chance of such. Meantime, there was *some* hope of our meeting *some*where on the road, but it was of the faintest. She thanked me feelingly for the interest I took in her own fated race, and gave

* Henry Schoolcraft, Esq.

me excellent hints as to my manner of proceeding. We were in the full tide of conversation when the bell of the steam-boat rang for the last time, and I was hurried off. On the deck of the vessel I found her husband, Mr. MacMurray, who had only time to say, in fewest words, all that was proper, polite, and hospitable. This rencontre, which some would call accidental, and some providential, pleased and encouraged me, and I felt very grateful to Dr. Rees.

Then came blessings, good wishes, kind pressures of the hand, and last adieus, and waving of handkerchiefs from the shore, as the paddles were set in motion, and we glided swiftly over the mirror-like bay, while "there was not a breath the blue waves to curl."

I had not been happy enough in Toronto to regret it as a place; and if touched, as I truly was, by the kind solicitude of those friends who, but a few weeks ago, were entire strangers to me, I yet felt no sorrow. Though no longer young, I am quite young enough to feel all the excitement of plunging into scenes so entirely new as were now opening before me; and this, too, with a specific object far beyond mere amusement and excitement—an object not unworthy.

But though the spirit was willing and cheerful, I was under the necessity of remembering that I was not all spirit, but clogged with a material frame which required some looking after. My general health had suffered during the long trying winter, and it was judiciously suggested that I should spend a fortnight at the falls of Niagara to recruit, previous to my journey. The good sense of this advice I could not appreciate at the time, any more than I could anticipate the fatigues and difficulties which awaited me; but my good angel, in the shape of a certain languid inclination for silence and repose, whispered me to listen and obey—fortunately, or providentially. Meantime I was alone—alone—and on my way to that ultimate somewhere of which I knew nothing, with forests, and plains, and successive seas intervening. The day was sultry, the air heavy and still, and a strange fog, or rather a series of dark clouds, hung resting on the bosom of the lake, which in some places was smooth and transparent as glass—in others, little eddies of wind had ruffled it into tiny waves, or welts rather—so that it presented the appearance of patchwork. The boatmen looked up and foretold a storm; but when we came within three or four miles from the mouth of the river Niagara, the fog drew off like a curtain, and the interminable line of the dark forest came into view, stretching right and left along the whole horizon; then the white buildings of the American fort, and the spires of the town of Niagara, became visible against the rich purple-green back-ground and we landed after a four hours' voyage. The threatened storm came on that night. The summer storms of Canada are like those of the tropic; not in Italy, not among the Appenines, where I have in my time heard the "live thunder leaping from crag to crag," did I ever hear such terrific explosions of sound as burst over our heads this night. The silence and the darkness lent an added horror to the elemental tumult—and for the first time in my life I felt sickened and unpleasantly affected in the intervals between the thunder-claps, though I cannot say I felt fear. Meantime the rain fell as in a deluge, threatening to wash us into the lake, which reared itself up, and roared—like a monster for its prey.

After several pleasant and interesting visits to the neighboring settlers, I took leave of my hospitable friends at Blandford with deep and real regret; and, in the best and only vehicle which could be procured—videlicet, a baker's cart—set out for London, the chief town of the district; the distance being about thirty miles—a long day's journey; the cost seven dollars.

The man who drove me proved a very intelligent and civilized person. He had come out to Canada in the capacity of a gentleman's servant; he now owned some land—I forget how many acres—and was besides baker-general for a large neighborhood, rarely receiving money in pay, but wheat and other farm produce. He had served as constable of the district for two years, and gave me some interesting accounts of his thief-taking expeditions through the wild forests in the deep winter nights. He considered himself, on the whole, a prosperous man. He said he should be quite happy here, were it not for his wife, who fretted and pined continually after her "home."

"But," said I, "surely wherever you are, is her *home*, and she ought to be happy where she sees you getting on better, and enjoying more of comfort and independence than you could have hoped to obtain in the old country."

"Well, yes," said he, hesitatingly; "and I can't say but that my wife is a good woman: I've no particular fault to find with her; and it's very natural she should mope, for she has no friend or acquaintance, you see, and she doesn't take to the people, and the ways here; and at home she had her mother and her sister to talk to; they lived with us, you see. Then, I'm out all day long, looking after my business, and she feels quite lonely like, and she's a crying when I come back—and I'm sure I don't know what to do!"

The case of this poor fellow with his discontented wife is no unfrequent occurrence in Canada; and among the better class of settlers the matter is worse still, the suffering more acute, and of graver consequences.

I have not often in my life met with contented and cheerful-minded women, but I never met with so many repining and discontented women as in Canada. I never met with *one* woman recently settled here, who considered herself happy in her new home and country: I *heard* of one, and doubtless there are others, but they are exceptions to the general rule. Those born here, or brought here early by their parents and relations, seemed to me very happy, and many of them had adopted a sort of pride in their new country, which I liked much. There was always a great desire to visit England, and some little airs of self-complacency and superiority in those who had been there, though for a few months only; but all, without a single exception, returned with pleasure, unable to forego the early habitual influences of their native land.

I like patriotism and nationality in women. Among the German women both these feelings give a strong tincture to the character; and, seldom disunited, they blend with peculiar grace in our sex: but with a great statesman they should stand well distinguished. Nationality is not always patriotism, and patriotism is not, necessarily, nationality. The English are more patriotic than national; the Americans generally more national than patriotic; the Germans both national and patriotic.

I have observed that really accomplished women, accustomed to what is called the best society, have more resources here, and manage better, than some women who have no pretensions of any kind, and whose claims to social distinction could not have been great any where, but whom I found lamenting over themselves as if they had been so many exiled princesses.

Can you imagine the position of a fretful, frivolous woman, strong neither in mind nor frame, abandoned to her own resources in the wilds of Upper Canada? I do not believe you *can* imagine any thing so pitiable, so ridiculous, and, to borrow the Canadian word, "so shiftless."

My new friend and kind hostess was a being of quite a different stamp; and though I believe she was far from thinking that she had found in Canada a terrestrial paradise, and the want of servants and the difficulty of educating her family as she wished, were subjects of great annoyance to her, yet these and other evils she had met with a cheerful spirit. Here, amid these forest wilds, she had recently given birth to a lovely baby, the tenth, or indeed I believe the twelfth of a flock of manly boys and blooming girls. Her eldest daughter meantime, a fair and elegant girl, was acquiring, at the age of fifteen, qualities and habits which might well make ample amends for the possessing of mere accomplishments. She acted as a manager-in-chief, and glided about in her household avocations with a serene and quiet grace which was quite charming.

The road, after leaving Woodstock, pursued the course of the winding Thames. We passed by the house of Colonel Light, in a situation of superlative natural beauty on a rising-ground above the river. A lawn, tolerably cleared, sloped down to the margin, while the opposite shore rose clothed in varied woods which had been managed with great taste, and a feeling for the picturesque not common here; but the Colonel being himself an accomplished artist accounts for this. We also passed Beechville, a small, but beautiful village, round which the soil is reckoned very fine and fertile; a number of most respectable settlers have recently bought land and erected houses here. The next place we came to was Oxford, or rather, Ingersol, where we stopped to dine and rest previous to plunging into an extensive forest, called the Pine Woods.

Oxford is a little village, presenting the usual saw-mill, grocery-store and tavern, with a dozen shanties congregated on the bank of the stream, which is here rapid and confined by high banks. Two back-woodsmen were in deep consultation over a wagon which had broken down in the midst of that very forest road we were about to traverse, and which they described as most execrable—in some parts even dangerous. As it was necessary to gird up my strength for the undertaking, I laid in a good dinner, consisting of slices of dried venison, broiled; hot cakes of Indian corn, eggs, butter, and a bowl of milk. Of this good fare I partook in company with the two back-woodsmen, who appeared to me perfect specimens of their class—tall and strong, and bronzed and brawny, and shaggy and unshaven—very much like two bears set on their hind legs; rude but not uncivil, and spare of speech, as men who had lived long at a distance from their kind. They were too busy, however, and so was I, to feel or express any mutual curiosity; time was valuable, appetite urgent—so we discussed our venison-steaks in silence, and after dinner I proceeded.

The forest land through which I had lately passed, was principally covered with *hard timber*, as oak, walnut, elm, basswood. We were now in a forest of pines, rising tall and dark, and monotonous on either side. The road worse certainly "than fancy ever feigned or fear conceived," put my neck in perpetual jeopardy. The driver had often to dismount, and partly fill up some tremendous hole with boughs before we could pass—or drag or lift the wagon over trunks of trees—or we sometimes sank into abysses, from which it is a wonder to me that we *ever* emerged. A natural question was—why did you not get out and walk?—Yes indeed! I only wish it had been possible. Immediately on the border of the road so called, was the wild, tangled, untrodden thicket, as impervious to the foot as the road was impassable, rich with vegetation, variegated verdure, and flowers of loveliest dye, but the haunt of the rattlesnake, and all manner of creeping and living things not pleasant to encounter, or even to think of.

The mosquitos, too, began to be troublesome; but not being yet in full force, I contrived to defend myself pretty well, by waving a green branch before me whenever my two hands were not employed in forcible endeavors to keep my seat. These seven miles of pine forests we traversed in three hours and a half; and then succeeded some miles of open flat country called the oak plains, and so called because covered with thickets and groups of oak, dispersed with a park-like and beautiful effect; and still flowers, flowers every where. The soil appeared sandy, and not so rich as in other parts.* The road was comparatively good, and as we approached London, clearing new settlements appeared on every side.

The sun had set amid a tumultuous mass of lurid threatening clouds, and a tempest was brooding in the air, when I reached the town, and found very tolerable accommodations in the principal inn. I was so terribly bruised and beaten with fatigue, that to move was impossible, and even to speak, too great an effort. I cast my weary aching limbs upon the bed, and requested of the very civil and obliging young lady who attended to bring me some books and newspapers. She brought me thereupon an old compendium of geography, published at Philadelphia forty years ago, and three newspapers. Two of these, the London Gazette and the Freeman's Journal, are printed and published within the district; the third, the New-York Albion, I have already mentioned to you as having been my delight and consolation at Toronto. This paper, an extensive double folio, is compiled for the use of the British settlers in the United States, and also in Canada, where it is widely circulated. It contains all the interesting public news in extracts from the leading English journals, with tales, essays, reviews, &c., from the periodicals. Think, now, if I had not reason to bless newspapers and civilization! Imagine me alone in the very centre of this vast wild country, a storm raging without, as if heaven and earth had come in collision—lodged and cared for, reclining on a neat comfortable bed, and reading by the light of one tallow candle (for there was a scarcity either of candles or of candlesticks), Sergeant Talfourd's speech in the Commons for the alteration of the law of copyright, given at full length, and if I had been worse than "kilt entirely," his noble eulogy of Wordsworth responded to by the cheers of the whole house, would have brought me to life; so did it make my very heart glow with approving sympathy.

* It is not the most open land which is most desirable for a settler. "The land," says Dr. Dunlop in his admirable little book, "is rich and lasting, just in proportion to the size and quantity of the timber which it bears, and therefore the more trouble he is put to it in clearing his land, the better will it repay him the labor he has expended on it."

July 5.

The next morning the weather continued very lowering and stormy. I wrote out my little journal for you carefully thus far, and then I received several visiters, who hearing of my arrival, had come with kind offers of hospitality and attention, such as are most grateful to a solitary stranger. I had also much conversation relative to the place and people, and the settlements around, and then I took a long walk about the town, of which I here give you the results.

When Governor Simcoe was planning the foundation of a capital for the whole province, he fixed at first upon the present site of London, struck by its many and obvious advantages. Its central position, in the midst of these great lakes, being at an equal distance from Huron, Erie, and Ontario, in the finest and most fertile district of the whole province, on the bank of a beautiful stream, and at a safe distance from the frontier, all pointed it out as the most eligible site for a metropolis; but there was the want of land and water communication—a want which still remains the only drawback to its rising prosperity. A canal or rail-road, running from Toronto and Hamilton to London, then branching off on the right to the harbor of Goderich on Lake Huron, and on the left to Sandwich on Lake Erie, were a glorious thing!—the one thing needful to make this fine country the granary and storehouse of the west; for here all grain, all fruits which flourish in the south of Europe, might be cultivated with success—the finest wheat and rice, and hemp and flax, and tobacco. Yet, in spite of this want, soon, I trust, to be supplied, the town of London has sprung up and become within ten years a place of great importance. In size and population it exceeds every town I have yet visited, except Toronto and Hamilton. The first house was erected in 1827; it now contains more than two hundred frame or brick houses; and there are many more building. The population may be about thirteen hundred people. The jail and court-house, comprised in one large stately edifice, seemed the glory of the townspeople. As for the style of architecture, I may not attempt to name or describe it; but a gentleman informed me, in rather equivocal phrase, that it was "*somewhat gothic.*" There are five places of worship, for the Episcopalians, Presbyterians,

Methodists, Roman Catholics, and Baptists. The church is handsome. There are also three or four schools, and seven taverns. The Thames is very beautiful here, and navigable for boats and barges. I saw to-day a large timber raft floating down the stream, containing many thousand feet of timber. On the whole, I have nowhere seen such evident signs of progress and prosperity.

The population consists principally of artisans—as blacksmiths, carpenters, builders, all flourishing. There is, I fear, a good deal of drunkenness and profligacy; for though the people have work and wealth, they have neither education nor amusements.* Besides the seven taverns, there is a number of little grocery-stores, which are, in fact, drinking-houses. And though a law exists, which forbids the sale of spirituous liquors in small quantities by any but licensed publicans, they easily contrive to elude the law; as thus:—a customer enters the shop, and asks for two or three pennyworth of nuts, or cakes, and he receives a few nuts, and a large glass of whiskey. The whiskey, you observe, is given, not sold, and no one can swear to the contrary. In the same manner the severe law against selling intoxicating liquors to the poor Indians is continually eluded or violated, and there is no redress for the injured, no punishment to reach the guilty. It appears to me that the government should be more careful in the choice of the district magistrates. While I was in London, a person who had acted in this capacity was carried from the pavement dead drunk.

Here, as every where else, I find the women of the better class lamenting over the want of all society, except of the

* Hear Dr. Channing, the wise and the good:—"People," he says, "should be guarded against temptation to unlawful pleasures by furnishing the means of innocent ones. In every community, there *must* be pleasures, relaxations, and means of agreeable excitement; and if innocent are not furnished, resort will be had to criminal. Man was made to enjoy as well as to labor; and the state of society should be adapted to this principle of human nature." "Men drink to excess very often to shake off depression, or to satisfy the restless thirst for agreeable excitement, and these motives are excluded in a cheerful community."

When I was in Upper Canada, I found no means whatever of social amusement for any class, except that which the tavern afforded; taverns consequently abounded every where.

lowest grade in manners and morals. For those who have recently emigrated, and are settled more in the interior, there is absolutely no social intercourse whatever; it is quite out of the question. They seem to me perishing of ennui, or from the want of sympathy which they cannot obtain, and, what is worse, which they cannot feel; for being in general unfitted for out-door occupations, unable to comprehend or enter into the interests around them, and all their earliest prejudices and ideas of the fitness of things continually outraged in a manner exceedingly unpleasant, they may be said to live in a perpetual state of inward passive discord and fretful endurance—

> "All too timid and reserved
> For onset, for resistance too inert—
> Too weak for suffering, and for hope too tame."

A gentleman, well known to me by name, who was not a resident in London, but passing through it on his way from a far western settlement up by Lake Huron, was one of my morning visiters. He had been settled in the Bush for five years, had a beautiful farm, well cleared, well stocked. He was pleased with his prospects, his existence, his occupations: all he wanted was a wife, and on this subject he poured forth a most eloquent appeal.

"Where," said he, "shall I find such a wife as I could, with a safe conscience, bring into these wilds, to share a settler's fate, a settler's home? You, who know your own sex so well, point me out such a one, or tell me at least where to seek her. I am perishing and deteriorating, head and heart, for want of a companion—a wife, in short. I am becoming as rude and coarse as my own laborers, and as hard as my own axe. If I wait five years longer, no woman will be able to endure such a fellow as I shall be by that time—no woman, I mean, whom I could marry—for in this lies my utter unreasonableness; habituated to seek in woman those graces and refinements which I have always associated with her idea, I must have them here in the forest, or dispense with all female society whatever. With some one to sympathize with me—to talk to—to embellish the home I return to at night—such a life as I now lead, with all the cares and frivolities of a too artificial society cast behind us, security and plenty all around us, and nothing but hope before us, a life of 'cheerful yesterdays and confident to-morrows'—were it not delicious? I want for myself nothing more, nothing better; but—perhaps it is a weakness, an inconsistency!—I could not love a woman who was inferior to all my preconceived notions of feminine elegance and refinement—inferior to my own mother and sisters. You know I was in England two years ago;—well, I have a vision of a beautiful creature, with the figure of a sylph and the head of a sibyl, beinding over her harp, and singing '*A te, O cara;*' and when I am logging in the woods with my men, I catch myself meditating on that vision, and humming *A te, O cara*, which somehow or other runs strangely in my head. Now, what is to be done? What could I do with that fair vision here? Without coxcombry may I not say, that I need not entirely despair of winning the affections of an amiable, elegant woman, and might even persuade her to confront, for my sake, worse than all this? For what will not your sex do and dare for the sake of us men creatures, savages that we are? But even for that reason shall I take advantage of such sentiments? You know what this life is—this isolated life in the Bush—and so do I; but by what words could I make it comprehensible to a fine lady? Certainly I might draw such a picture of it as should delight by its novelty and romance, and deceive even while it does not deviate from the truth. A cottage in the wild woods—solitude and love—the world forgetting, by the world forgot—the deer come skipping by—the red Indian brings game, and lays it at her feet—how pretty and how romantic! And for the first few months, perhaps the first year, all goes well; but how goes it the next, and the next? I have observed with regard to the women who come out, that they do well enough the first year, and some even the second; but the third is generally fatal: and the worst with you women—or the best shall I not say?—is, that you cannot, and do not, forget domestic ties left behind. We men go out upon our land, or to the chase, and the women, poor souls, sit, and sew, and *think*. You have seen Mrs. A. and Mrs. B., who came out here, as I well remember, full of health and bloom—what are they now? premature old women, sickly, care-worn, without nerve or cheerfulness:—and as for C——, who brought his wife to his place by Lake Simcoe only three years ago, I hear the poor fellow must sell all off, or see his wife perish before his eyes. Would you have me risk the alternative? Or perhaps you will say, marry one of the women of the country—one of the daughters *of the Bush.* No, I cannot; I must have something different. I may not have been particularly fortunate, but the women I have seen are in general coarse and narrow minded, with no education whatever, or with an education which apes all I most dislike, and omits all I could admire in the fashionable education of the old country. What could I do with such women? In the former I might find an upper servant, but no companion—in the other, neither companionship nor help!"

To this discontented and fastidious gentleman I ventured to recommend two or three very amiable girls I had known at Toronto and Niagara; and I told him, too, that among the beautiful and spirited girls of New-England, he might also find what would answer his purpose. But with regard to Englishwomen of that grade in station and education, and personal attraction, which would content him, I could not well speak; not because I knew of none who united grace of person and lively talents with capabilities of strong affection, ay, and sufficient energy of character to meet trials and endure privations; but in women, as now educated, there is a strength of local habits and attachments, a want of cheerful self-dependence, a cherished physical delicacy, a weakness of temperament,—deemed, and falsely deemed, in deference to the pride of man, essential to feminine grace and refinement,—altogether unfitting them for a life which were otherwise delightful:—the active out-of-door life in which she must share and sympathize, and the in-door occupations which in England are considered servile; for a woman who cannot perform for herself and others all household offices, has no business here. But when I hear some men declare that they cannot endure to see women eat, and others speak of brilliant health and strength in young girls as being rude and vulgar, with various notions of the same kind too grossly absurd and perverted even for ridicule, I cannot wonder at any nonsensical affectations I meet within my own sex; nor do otherwise than pity the mistakes and deficiencies of those who are sagely brought up with the one end and aim—to get married. As you always used to say, "Let there be a demand for a better article, and a better article will be supplied."

The plan of travel I had laid down for myself did not permit of my making any long stay in London. I was anxious to push on to the Talbot Settlement, or, as it is called here, the Talbot *Country*, a name not ill applied to a vast tract of land stretching from east to west along the shore of Lake Erie, and of which Colonel Talbot is the sovereign *de facto*, if not *de jure*—be it spoken without any derogation to the rights of our lord the king. This immense settlement, the circumstances to which it owed its existence, and the character of the eccentric man who founded it on such principles as have insured its success and prosperity, altogether inspired me with the strongest interest and curiosity.

To the residence of this "big chief," as an Indian styled him—a solitary mansion on a cliff above Lake Erie, where he lived alone in his glory—was I now bound, without exactly knowing what reception I was to meet there, for that was a point which the despotic habits and eccentricities of this hermit-lord of the forest rendered a little doubtful. The reports I had heard of his singular manners, of his being a sort of woman-hater, who had not for thirty years allowed a female to appear in his sight, I had partly discredited, yet enough remained to make me feel a little nervous. However, my resolution was taken, and the colonel had been apprized of my intended visit, though of his gracious acquiescence I was yet to learn; so, putting my trust in Providence, as heretofore, I prepared to encounter the old buffalo in his lair.

From the master of the inn at London I hired a vehicle and a driver for eight dollars. The distance was about thirty miles; the road, as my Irish informant assured me, was quite "iligant!" but hilly, and so broken by the recent storms, that it was thought I could not reach my destination before nightfall, and I was advised to sleep at the little town of St. Thomas, about twelve or fifteen miles on this side of Port Talbot. However, I was resolute to try, and, with a pair of stout horses and a willing driver, did not despair. My conveyance from Blandford had been a baker's cart on springs; but springs were a luxury I was in future to dispense with. My present vehicle, the best to be procured, was a common cart, with straw at the bottom; in the midst a seat was suspended on straps, and furnished with a cushion, not of the softest. A board nailed across the front served for the driver, a quiet, demure-looking boy of fifteen or sixteen, with a round straw hat and a fustian jacket. Such was the elegant and appropriate equipage in which the "chancellor's lady," as they call me here, paid her first visit of state to the "great Colonel Talbot."

Route of Anna Jameson's Summer Rambles, June–August 1837

SUMMER RAMBLES IN CANADA

——————— *You shall*
Go forth upon your arduous task alone,
None shall assist you, none partake your toil,
None share your triumph! still you must retain
Some one to trust your glory to—to share
Your rapture with.

PARACELSUS

Port Talbot, July 10.

"Man is, properly speaking, based upon hope. He has no other possession but hope. This world of his is emphatically the place of hope:"* and more emphatically than of any other spot on the face of the globe, it is true of this new world of ours, in which I am now a traveller and a sojourner. This is the land of hope, of faith, ay, and of charity, for a man who hath not all three had better not come here; with them he may, by strength of his own right hand and trusting heart, achieve miracles: witness Colonel Talbot.

Of the four days in which I have gone wandering and wondering up and down, let me now tell you something—*all* I cannot tell you; for the information I have gained, and the reflections and feelings which have passed through my mind, would fill a volume—and I have little time for scribbling.

And first of Colonel Talbot himself. This remarkable man is now about sixty-five, perhaps more, but he does not look so much. In spite of his rustic dress, his good-humored, jovial, weather-beaten face, and the primitive simplicity, not to say rudeness, of his dwelling, he has in his features, air, and deportment, that *something* which stamps him gentleman. And that *something* which thirty-four years of solitude has not effaced, he derives, I suppose, from blood and birth, things of more consequence, when philosophically and philanthropically considered, than we are apt to allow. He must have been very handsome when young; his resemblance now to our royal family, particularly to the King (William the Fourth), is so very striking as to be something next to identity. Good-natured people have set themselves to account for this wonderful likeness in various ways, possible and impossible; but after a rigid comparison of dates and ages, and assuming all that latitude which scandal usually allows herself in these matters, it remains unaccountable, unless we suppose that the Talbots have, *par la grace de Dieu*, a family knack of resembling kings. You may remember that the extraordinary resemblance which his ancestor Dick Talbot (Duke of Tyrconnel) bore to Louis the Four-

* *Vide* Sartor Resartus.

teenth, gave occasion to the happiest and most memorable repartee ever recorded in the chronicle of wit.*

Colonel Talbot came out to Upper Canada as aide-de-camp to Governor Simcoe in 1793, and accompanied the governor on the first expedition he made to survey the western district, in search (as it was said) of an eligible site for the new capital he was then projecting. At this time the whole of the beautiful and fertile region situated between the lakes was a vast wilderness. It contained not one white settler, except along the borders, and on the coast opposite to Detroit: a few wandering tribes of Hurons and Chippewas, and the Six Nations settled on Grand River, were its only inhabitants.

It was then that the idea of founding a colony took possession of Col. Talbot's mind, and became the ruling passion and sole interest of his future life. For this *singular* project, wise people have set themselves to account much in the same manner as for his likeness to William the Fourth. That a man of noble birth, high in the army, young and handsome, and eminently qualified to shine in society, should voluntarily banish himself from all intercourse with the civilized world, and submit, not for a temporary frolic, but for long tedious years, to the most horrible privations of every kind, appeared too incomprehensible to be attributed to any of the ordinary motives and feelings of a reasonable human being; so they charitably set it down to motives and feelings very extraordinary indeed,—and then "they looked the lie they dared not speak." Others went no farther than to insinuate or assert that early in life he had met with a disappointment in love, which had turned his brain. I had always heard and read of him, as the "eccentric" Colonel Talbot. Of his eccentricity I heard much more than of his benevolence, his invincible courage, his enthusiasm, his per-

* As it is just possible that the reader may not have met with this anecdote, it is here repeated—perhaps for the thousandth time: When Richard Talbot was sent ambassador to France, the king, struck by that likeness to himself which had excited the attention of his courtiers, addressed him on some occasion, "M. l'Ambassadeur, est-ce que madame votre mère a jamais été dans la cour du Roi mon père?" Talbot replied with a low bow, "Non, sire—mais mon père y était!"

severance; but perhaps, according to the worldly nomenclature, these qualities come under the general head of "eccentricity," when devotion to a favourite object cannot possibly be referred to self-interest.

On his return to England, he asked and obtained a grant of 100,000 acres of land along the shores of Lake Erie, on condition of placing a settler on every two hundred acres He came out again in 1802, and took possession of his domain, in the heart of the wilderness. Of the life he led for the first sixteen years, and the difficulties and obstacles he encountered, he drew, in his discourse with me, a strong, I might say a *terrible* picture: and observe that it was not a life of wild wandering freedom—the life of an Indian hunter, which is said to be so fascinating that "no man who has ever followed it for any length of time, *ever* voluntarily returns to civilized society!"* Col. Talbot's life has been one of persevering, heroic self-devotion to the completion of a magnificent plan, laid down in the first instance, and followed up with unflinching tenacity of purpose. For sixteen years he saw scarce a human being, except the few boors and blacks employed in clearing and logging his land: he himself assumed the blanket-coat and axe, slept upon the bare earth, cooked three meals a day for twenty woodsmen, cleaned his own boots, washed his own linen, milked his cows, churned the butter, and made and baked the bread. In this latter branch of household economy he became very expert, and still piques himself on it.

To all these heterogeneous functions of sowing and reaping, felling and planting, frying, boiling, washing, wringing, brewing, and baking, he added another, even more extraordinary;—for many years he solemnized all the marriages in his district!

While Europe was converted into a vast battlefield, an arena

> "Where distract ambition compassed
> And was encompass'd,"

and his brothers in arms, the young men who had begun the career of life with him, were reaping bloody laurels, to be gazetted in the list of killed and wounded, as heroes—then

* Dr. Dunlop.

forgotten;—Col. Talbot, a true hero after another fashion, was encountering, amid the forest solitude, uncheered by sympathy, unbribed by fame, enemies far more formidable, and earning a far purer, as well as a more real and lasting immortality.

Besides natural obstacles, he met with others far more trying to his temper and patience. His continual quarrels with the successive governors, who were jealous of the independent power he exercised in his own territory, are humorously alluded to by Dr. Dunlop.

"After fifteen years of unremitting labour and privation," says the Doctor, "it became so notorious in the province, that even the executive government at Toronto became aware that there was such a place as the Talbot Settlement, where roads were cut and farms in progress; and hereupon they rejoiced—for it held out to them just what they had long felt the want of, a well-settled, opened, and cultivated country, wherein to obtain estates for themselves, their children, born and unborn, and their whole kith, kin, and allies. When this idea, so creditable to the paternal feelings of these worthy gentlemen, was intimated to the Colonel, he could not be brought to see the fitness of things in an arrangement which would confer on the next generation, or the next again, the fruits of the labour of the present; and accordingly, though his answer to the proposal was not couched in terms quite so diplomatic as might have been wished, it was brief, soldier-like, and not easily capable of misconstruction; it was in these words—"I'll be d—d if you get one foot of land here;" and thereupon the parties joined issue.

"On this, war was declared against him by his Excellency in council, and every means were used to annoy him here, and misrepresent his proceedings at home; but he stood firm, and by an occasional visit to the colonial office in England, he opened the eyes of ministers to the proceedings of both parties, and for a while averted the danger. At length, some five years ago, finding the enemy was getting too strong for him, he repaired once more to England, and returned in triumph with an order from the Colonial Office, that nobody was in any way to interfere with his proceedings; and he has now the pleasure of contemplating some hundreds of miles of the best roads in the province, closely settled on each side by the most prosperous farmers within its bounds, who owe all they possess to his judgment, enthusiasm, and perseverance, and who are grateful to him in proportion to the benefits he has bestowed upon them, though in many instances sorely against their will at the time."

The original grant must have been much extended, for the territory now under Colonel Talbot's management, and bearing the general name of the Talbot Country, contains, according to the list I have in his own handwriting, twenty-eight townships, and about 650,000 acres of land, of which 98,700 are cleared and cultivated. The inhabitants, including the population of the towns, amount to about 50,000. "You see," said he gaily, "I may boast, like the Irishman in the farce, of having peopled a whole country with my own hands."

He has built his house, like the eagle his eyry, on a bold high cliff overhanging the lake. On the east there is a precipitous descent into a wild woody ravine, along the bottom of which winds a gentle stream, till it steals into the lake: this stream is in winter a raging torrent. The storms and the gradual action of the waves have detached large portions of the cliff in front of the house, and with them huge trees. Along the lake-shore I found trunks and roots of trees half-buried in the sand, or half-overflowed with water, which I often mistook for rocks. I remember one large tree, which, in falling headlong, still remained suspended by its long and strong fibres to the cliff above; its position was now reversed—the top hung downwards, shivered and denuded: the large spread root, upturned, formed a platform, on which new earth had accumulated, and a new vegetation sprung forth, of flowers, and bushes, and sucklings. Altogether it was a most picturesque and curious object.

Lake Erie, as the geography book says, is two hundred and eighty miles long, and here, at Port Talbot, which is near the centre, about seventy miles across. The Colonel tells me that it has been more than once frozen over from side to side, but I do not see how this fact could be ascertained, as no one has been known to cross to the opposite shore on the ice. It is true that more ice accumulates in this lake than in any other of the great lakes, by reason of its shallowness; it can be sounded through its whole extent, while the other lakes are found in some parts unfathomable.

But to return to the chateau: it is a long wooden building, chiefly of rough logs, with a covered porch running along the south side. Here I found suspended, among sundry implements of husbandry, one of those ferocious animals of the feline kind, called here the cat-a-mountain, and by some the American tiger, or panther, which it more resembles. This one, which had been killed in its attack on the fold or poultry-yard, was at least four feet in length, and glared on me from the rafters above, ghastly and horrible. The interior of the house contains several comfortable lodging-rooms; and one really handsome one, the dining-room. There is a large kitchen with a tremendously hospitable chimney, and underground are cellars for storing wine, milk and provisions. Around the house stands a vast variety of outbuildings, of all imaginable shapes and sizes, and disposed without the slightest regard to order or symmetry. One of these is the very log-hut which the Colonel erected for shelter when he first "sat down in the bush," four-and-thirty years ago, and which he is naturally unwilling to remove. Many of these outbuildings are to shelter the geese and poultry, of which he rears an innumerable quantity. Beyond these is the cliff, looking over the wide blue lake, on which I have counted six schooners at a time with their white sails; on the left is Port Stanley. Behind the house lies an open tract of land, prettily broken and varied, where large flocks of sheep and cattle were feeding—the whole enclosed by beautiful and luxuriant woods, through which runs the little creek or river abovementioned.

The farm consists of six hundred acres: but as the Colonel is not quite so active as he used to be, and does not employ a bailiff or overseer, the management is said to be slovenly, and not so productive as it might be.

He has sixteen acres of orchard-ground, in which he has planted and reared with success all the common European fruits, as apples, pears, plums, cherries, in abundance; but what delighted me beyond everything else, was a garden of more than two acres, very neatly laid out and enclosed, and in which he evidently took exceeding pride and pleasure; it was the first thing he showed me after my arrival. It abounds in roses of different kinds, the cuttings of which he had brought himself from England in the few visits he had made there. Of these he gathered the most beautiful buds, and presented them to me with such an air as might have become Dick Talbot presenting a bouquet to Miss Jennings.* We then sat down on a pretty seat under a tree, where he told me he often came to meditate. He described the appearance of the spot when he first came here, as contrasted with its present appearance, or we discussed the exploits of some of his celebrated and gallant ancestors, with whom my acquaintance was (luckily) almost as intimate as his own. Family and aristocratic pride I found a prominent feature in the character of this remarkable man. A Talbot of Malahide, of a family representing the same barony from father to son for six hundred years, he set, not unreasonably, a high value on his noble and unstained lineage; and, in his lonely position, the simplicity of his life and manners lent to these lofty and not unreal pretensions a kind of poetical dignity.

I told him of the surmises of the people relative to his early life and his motives for emigrating, at which he laughed.

"Charlevoix," said he, "was, I believe, the true cause of my coming to this place. You know he calls this the 'Paradise of the Hurons.' Now I was resolved to get to paradise by hook or by crook, and so I came here."

He added, more seriously, "I have accomplished what I resolved to do—it is done. But I would not, if any one was to offer me the universe, go through again the *horrors* I have undergone in forming this settlement. But do not imagine I repent it; I like my retirement."

He then broke out against the follies and falsehoods and restrictions of artificial life, in bitter and scornful terms; no ascetic monk or *radical* philosopher could have been more eloquently indignant.

I said it was granted to few to live a life of such complete retirement, and at the same time such general utility; in flying from the world he had benefitted it: and I added, that I was glad to see him so happy.

"Why, yes, I'm very happy here"—and then the old man sighed.

* Dick Talbot married Frances Jennings—*la belle Jennings* of De Grammont's Memoirs, and elder sister of the celebrated Duchess of Marlborough.

I understood that sigh, and in my heart echoed it. No, "it is not good for man to be alone;" and this law, which the Father of all life pronounced himself at man's creation, was never yet violated with impunity. Never yet was the human being withdrawn from, or elevated above, the social wants and sympathies of his human nature, without paying a tremendous price for such isolated independence.

With all my admiration for what this extraordinary man has achieved, and the means, the powers, through which he has achieved it, there mingles a feeling of commiseration, which has more than once brought the tears to my eyes while listening to him. He had passed his life in worse than solitude. He will admit no equal in his vicinity. His only intercourse has been with inferiors and dependents, whose servility he despised, and whose resistance enraged him—men whose interests rested on his favour—on his will, from which there was no appeal. Hence despotic habits, and contempt even for those whom he benefitted: hence, with much natural benevolence and generosity, a total disregard, or rather total ignorance, of the feelings of others;—all the disadvantages, in short, of royalty, only on a smaller scale. Now, in his old age, where is to him the solace of age? He has honour, power, obedience; but where are the love, the troops of friends, which also should accompany old age? He is alone—a lonely man. His constitution has suffered by the dreadful toils and privations of his earlier life. His sympathies have had no natural outlet, his affections have wanted their natural food. He suffers, I think; and not being given to general or philosophical reasoning, causes and effects are felt, not known. But he is a great man who has done great things, and the good which he has done will live after him. He has planted, at a terrible sacrifice, an enduring name and fame, and will be commemorated in this "brave new world," this land of hope, as Triptolemus among the Greeks.

For his indifference or dislike to female society, and his determination to have no settler within a certain distance of his own residence, I could easily account when I knew the man; both seemed to me the natural result of certain habits of life acting upon a certain organization. He has a favourite servant, Jeffrey by name, who has served him faithfully for more than five-and-twenty years, ever since he left off cleaning his own shoes and mending his own coat. This honest fellow, not having forsworn female companionship, began to sigh after a wife —

> "A wife! ah! Saint Marie Benedicité
> How might a man have any adversité
> That hath a wife?"

And, like the good knight in Chaucer, he did

> "Upon his bare knees pray God him to send
> A wife to last unto his life's end."

So one morning he went and took unto himself the woman nearest at hand—one, of whom we must needs suppose that he chose her for her virtues, for most certainly it was not for her attractions. The Colonel swore at him for a fool; but, after a while, Jeffrey, who is a favorite, smuggled his wife into the house; and the Colonel, whose increasing age renders him rather more dependent on household help, seems to endure very patiently this addition to his family, and even the presence of a white-headed chubby little thing, which I found running about without let or hindrance.

The room into which I first introduced you, with its rough log-walls, is Colonel Talbot's library and hall of audience. On leaving my apartment in the morning, I used to find groups of strange figures lounging round the door. ragged, black-bearded, gaunt, travel-worn and toil-worn emigrants, Irish, Scotch, and American, come to offer themselves as settlers. These he used to call his land-pirates; and curious, and characteristic, and dramatic beyond description, were the scenes which used to take place between this grand bashaw of the wilderness and his hungry, importunate clients and petitioners.

Another thing which gave a singular interest to my conversations with Colonel Talbot, was the sort of indifference with which he regarded all the stirring events of the last thirty years. Dynasties rose and disappeared; kingdoms were passed from hand to hand like wine decanters; battles were lost and won;—he neither knew, nor heard, nor cared. No post, no newspaper brought to his forest-hut the tidings of victory and defeat, of revolutions of empires, "of rumours of unsuccessful and successful war."

When he first took to the bush, Napoleon was consul; when he emerged from his solitude, the tremendous game of ambition had been played out, and Napoleon and his deeds and his dynasty were numbered with the things o'er-past. With the stream of events had flowed by equally unmarked the stream of mind, thought, literature—the progress of social improvement—the changes in public opinion. Conceive what a gulf between us! but though I could go to him, he could not come to me—my sympathies had the wider range of the two.

The principal foreign and domestic events of his *reign* are the last American war, in which he narrowly escaped being taken prisoner by a detachment of the enemy, who ransacked his house, and drove off his horses and cattle; and a visit he received some years ago from three young Englishmen of rank and fortune, Lord Stanley, Mr. Stuart Wortley, and Mr. Labouchere, who spent some weeks with him. These events, and his voyages to England, seemed to be the epochs from which he dated. His last trip to England was about three years ago. From these occasional flights he returns like an old eagle to his perch on the cliff, whence he looks down upon the world he has quitted with supreme contempt and indifference, and around on that which he has created, with much self-applause and self-gratulation.

"Alles was Du siehst und so wei Du's siehst,—was Dir das Liebste, das Schrecklichste, das Peinlichste, das Heimlichste, das Verführerischeste ist, das kehre hervor—"

RAHEL.

It was not till the sixth day of my sojourn at Port Talbot that the good colonel could be persuaded to allow of my departure.

He told me, with good-humoured peremptoriness, that he was the grand autocrat of the forest, and that to presume to order horses, or take any step towards departing, without his express permission, was against "his laws." At last he was so good as to issue his commands—with flattering reluctance, however—that a vehicle should be prepared, and a trusty guide provided; and I bade farewell to this extraordinary man with a mixture of delighted, and grateful, and melancholy feelings not easily to be described, nor ever forgotten.

Detroit, June —.

The roads by which I have at length reached this beautiful little city were not certainly the smoothest and the easiest in the world; nor can it be said of Upper Canada as of wisdom, "that all her ways are ways of pleasantness, and her paths are paths of peace." On the contrary, one might have fancied oneself in the road to paradise for that matter. It was difficult, and narrow, and foul, and steep enough to have led to the seventh heaven; but in heaven I am not yet—

* * * *

Since my arrival at Detroit, some malignant planet reigns in place of that favorable and guiding star which has hitherto led me so deftly on my way,

"Through brake, through brier,
Through mud, through mire."

Here, where I expected all would go so well, everything goes wrong, and cross, and contrary.

A severe attack of illness, the combined effect of heat, fatigue, and some deleterious properties in the water at Detroit, against which travellers should be warned, has confined me to my room for the last three days. This *mal-apropos* indisposition has prevented me from taking my pasage in the great steamer which has just gone up Lake Huron; and I must now wait here six days longer, till the next boat bound for Mackinaw and Chicago, comes up Lake Erie from Buffalo. What is far worse, I have lost, for the time being, the advantage of seeing and knowing Daniel Webster, and of hearing a display of that wonderful eloquence which they say takes captive all ears, hearts, and souls. He has been making public speeches here, appealing to the people against the money transactions of the government; and the whole city has been in a ferment. He left Detroit two days after my arrival, to my no small mortification. I had letters for him; and it so happens that several others to whom I had also letters, have fled from the city on summer tours, or to escape the heat. Some have gone east, some west, some up the lakes, some down the lakes; so I am abandoned to my own resources in a miserable state of languor, lassitude, and weakness.

It is not, however, the first time I have had to endure sickness and solitude together in a strange land; and the worst being over, we must needs make the best of it, and send the time away as well as we can.

Of all the places I have yet seen in these far western regions, Detroit is the most interesting. It is, moreover, a most ancient and venerable place, dating back to the dark immemorial ages, *i.e.* almost a century and a quarter ago! and having its history and antiquities, and traditions and heroes, and epochs of peace and war. "No place in the United States presents such a series of events interesting in themselves, and permanently affecting, as they occurred, both its progress and prosperity. Five times its flag has changed; three different sovereignties have claimed its allegiance; and since it has been held by the United States, its government has been thrice transferred: twice it has been besieged by the Indians, once captured in war, and once burned to the ground:"—truly, a long list of events for a young city of a century old! Detroit may almost rival her old grandam Quebec, who sits bristling defiance on the summit of her rocky height, in warlike and tragic experience.

Can you tell me why we gave up this fine and important place to the Americans, without leaving ourselves even a fort on the opposite shore? Dolts and blockheads as we have been in all that concerns the partition and management of these magnificent regions, now that we have ignorantly and blindly ceded whole countries, and millions and millions of square miles of land and water to our neighbors, they say we are likely to quarrel and go to war about a partition line through the barren tracts of the east! Well, this is not your affair nor mine—let our legislators look to it. Colonel Talbot told me that when he took a map, and pointed out to one of the English commissioners the foolish bargain they had made, the real extent, value, and resources of the countries ceded to the United States, the man covered his eyes with his clenched hands, and burst into tears.

If you look upon the map, you will find that the Detroit River, so called, is rather a strait or channel about thirty miles in length, and in breadth from one to two or three miles, dividing the British from the American shore. Through this channel all the waters of the upper lakes, Michigan, Superior, and Huron, come pouring down on their way to the ocean. Here, at Detroit, the breadth of the river does not exceed a mile. A pretty little steamer, gaily painted, with streamers flying, and shaded by an awning, is continually passing and re-passing from shore to shore. I have sometimes sat in this ferry-boat for a couple of hours together, pleased to remain still, and enjoy, without exertion, the cool air, the sparkling redundant waters, and green islands:—amused, meantime by the variety and conversation of the passengers, English emigrants, and French Canadians; brisk Americans; dark, sad-looking Indians folded in their blankets; farmers, storekeepers, speculators in wheat; artisans; trim girls with black eyes and short petticoats, speaking a Norman *patois*, and bringing baskets of fruit to the Detroit market; over-dressed, long-waisted, damsels of the city, attended by their beaux, going to make merry on the opposite shore. The passage is not of more than ten minutes' duration, yet there is a tavern bar on the lower deck, and a constant demand for cigars, liquors, and mint julep—by the *men* only, I pray you to observe, and the Americans chiefly; I never saw the French peasants ask for drink.

Yesterday and to-day, feeling better, I have passed some hours straying or driving about on the British shore.

I hardly know how to convey to you an idea of the difference between the two shores; it will appear to you as incredible as it is to me incomprehensible. Our shore is said to be the most fertile, and has been the longest settled; but to float between them (as I did to-day in a little canoe made of a hollow tree, and paddled by a half-breed imp of a boy)—to behold on one side a city, with its towers and spires and animated population, with villas and handsome houses stretching along the shore, and a hundred vessels or more, gigantic steamers, brigs, schooners, crowding the port, loading and unloading; all the bustle, in short, of prosperity and commerce;—and, on the other side, a little straggling hamlet, one schooner, one little wretched steamboat, some windmills, a catholic chapel or two, a supine ignorant peasantry, all the symptoms of apathy, indolence, mistrust hopelessness!—can I, can any one, help wondering at the difference, and asking whence it arises? There must be a cause for it surely—but what is it? Does it lie in past or in present—in natural or accidental circumstances?—in the institutions of the government, or the character of the people? Is it remediable? is it a necessity? is it a mystery? what and whence is it?—Can you tell? or can you send some of our colonial officials across the Atlantic to behold and solve the difficulty?

The little hamlet opposite to Detroit is called Richmond. I was sitting there to-day on the grassy bank above the river, resting in the shade of a tree, and speculating on all these things, when an old French Canadian stopped near me to arrange something about his cart. We entered forthwith into conversation; and though I had some difficulty in making out his *patois*, he understood my French, and we got on very well. If you would see the two extremes of manner brought into near comparison, you should turn from a Yankee storekeeper to a French Canadian! It was quite curious to find in this remote region such a perfect specimen of an old-fashioned Norman peasant—all bows, courtesy, and good-humour. He was carrying a cart-load of cherries to Sandwich, and when I begged for a ride, the little old man bowed and smiled, and poured forth a voluble speech, in which the words *enchanté! honneur!* and *madame!* were all I could understand; but these were enough. I mounted the cart, seated myself in an old chair surrounded with baskets heaped with ripe cherries, lovely as those of Shenstone—

> "Scattering like blooming maid their glances round,
> And must be bought, though penury betide!"

No occasion, however, to risk penury here; for after permission asked, and granted with a pleasant smile and a hundredth removal of the ragged hat, I failed not to profit by my situation, and dipped my hand pretty frequently into these tempting baskets. When the French penetrated into these regions a century ago, they brought with them not only their national courtesy, but some of their finest national fruits,—plums, cherries, apples, pears, of the best quality—excellent grapes, too, I am told—and all these are now grown in such abundance as to be almost valueless. For his cart-load of cherries my old man expected a sum not exceeding two shillings.

Sandwich is about two miles below Detroit. It is the chief

place in the Western District, the county town; yet the population does not much exceed four hundred.

I had to regret much the absence of Mr. Prince, the great proprietor of the place, and a distinguished member of our House of Assembly, both for ability and eloquence; but I saw sufficient to convince me that Sandwich makes no progress. The appearance of the place and people, so different from all I had left on the opposite side of the river, made me melancholy, or rather thoughtful. What can be the reason that all flourishes *there*, and all languishes *here*?

Amherstberg, another village about ten miles farther, contains about six hundred inhabitants, has a good harbor, and all natural capabilities; but here also no progress is making. There is a wretched little useless fort, commanding, or rather not commanding, the entrance to the Detroit river on our side, and memorable in the history of the last American war as Fort Malden. There are here a few idle soldiers, detached from the garrison at Toronto; and it is said that even these will be removed. In case of an attack or sudden outbreak, all this exposed and important line of shore is absolutely without defence.*

Near Amherstberg there is a block of reserved land, about seven miles square, the property of a tribe of Huron or Wyandot Indians: it extends along the banks of the Detroit river, and is one of the finest regions for climate, soil, and advantages of every kind, in the whole province; of great importance too, as lying opposite to the American shore, and literally a stumbling-*block* in the way of the white settlements, diminishing very considerably the value and eligibility of the lands around. Our government has been frequently in negociation with these Indians to induce them to dispose of their lands, and I understand that fifteen thousand acres have lately been purchased from them. It is most certain, however, that in all these transactions they consider themselves aggrieved.

I have in my possession an original petition of these Wyandot Indians, addressed to Sir John Colborne. It appears that in 1829, the other lake tribes, the Chippewas, Pottowattomies, and Ottawas, claimed an equal right to these lands,

* This was written on the spot. Since the late troubles in Upper Canada, it is understood to be the intention of Sir John Colborne to fortify this coast.

and offered to dispose of them to our government. The Hurons resisted this claim, and were most unwilling to relinquish their right to keep and reside on their "own little piece of land." The petition, which has been translated by one of their missionaries in a style rather too ambitious and flowery, contains some very touching and beautiful passages. They open their statement of grievances thus:—

"FATHER!

"Your Red children the Hurons approach you under the gathering clouds of affliction. Father, we visit you to tell you the sorrows of our hearts. We have learned at a council that the three nations of Ottawas, Chippewas, and Pottowattomies, claim our lands. We understand, with grief and surprise, that they proposed at that council to traffic with you for our Huron reserve."

They then allude to their ancient contests with the Iroquois, by which they were driven up the lakes, as far as beyond Lake Michigan; and their return to their former hunting-grounds when these contests ceased.

"Our fires were quenched, and their ashes scattered: but, Father, we collected them again, removed to our present homes, and there rekindled the embers."

They allude to their services in the late war, as giving them a peculiar claim to protection.

"Father, when the war-hatchet was sent by our great Father to the Americans, we too raised it against them. Father, we fought your enemies on the very spot we now inherit. The pathway to our doors is red with our blood. Every track to our homes reminds us, 'here fell a brother'—fell, Father! in the hour of strife for you. But, Father, we mourn not for them. The memory of their exploits lives sacred in our breasts. We mourn not for them; we mourn for ourselves and our children. We would not recal them to the pains and sufferings through which the steps of the living Huron must pass. Theirs is the morning of stillness after the tempest: the day of peace after the fury of the battle! Father, their brave spirits look down upon you. By their blood we implore you to stretch your protecting arm over us. The war-club has been glutted with the havoc of our nation. We look round for our young men, our warriors, our chiefs: where is now the Huron? gone, Father, laid low in the earth; nerveless are now the hands that grasped the Huron tomahawk. Father, in our might we aided you: let us not lament in our weakness that our vigour has been wasted."

They then attempt to substantiate their claim by pointing out the places which bear their name, as the ancient inhabitants of the soil; and it is certain that in the time of Charlevoix all these regions were in possession of the Huron tribes.

"The great lake is called the *Huron* Lake. There are no less than three rivers in our vicinity which bear the name of the Huron: the Huron river on the north side of Lake St. Clair—the Huron river on the north side of Lake Erie—and the Huron river on the south side of Lake Erie. Upper and Lower Sandusky* owe their names to our language. Father, what is the soil in dispute everywhere termed? The Ottawa or Chippewa Reserve?—no, Father; but simply the Huron Reserve. Thus your maps designate it. We had a village at Big Rock, in the entrance to the westerly channel of the river Detroit, called Brown's Town, from one of our chiefs. Another at Maguaga, in the same channel. But Amherstberg now covers the space where were once our principal town and settlement, extending to the mouth of the river Des Canards, our present abode."

"Yet, Father, the Ottawas ask our lands as their property; they offer to you the sale of crops they have not tilled—of barns they have not raised—of houses they have not built—of homes wherein they never slept. Father, they would reap where the ancient Huron only has sown."

* * * *

"Father, we have had the strongest declarations that we should not be molested, from Governor Simcoe, on the behalf of our great Father; also from the Governor-general, Lord Dorchester; from Governor Gore, and from every other Governor to the present day. The same has been repeated to us by your commanding officers stationed at Amherstberg. Father, on the faith of these repeated promises, we retained our habitations among you. Deeming your protection certain, we have cleared our fields and cultivated them, raised barns for our grain, and houses for our families. We have taught

* Two rising towns on the American shore of Lake Erie.

our children to smoke the pipe of peace, and follow the precepts of the gospel. Our feet are unaccustomed to the chase —their swiftness is no more; our hands unfamiliar with the bow, and the sureness of the arrow is lost."

They attribute these new claims to their lands to the devices of their white neighbors, and they allude to their fallen state and diminished numbers as pleas for the white man's forbearance.

"We conjure you not to expel us from our homes, rendered dear to us by many recollections. The morning and the noonday of our nation has passed away—the evening is fast settling in darkness round us. It is hardly worth an effort to hasten the close of night," &c.

"Father, the dejected Huron throws himself upon your clemency and justice."

This petition is signed by their principal chief, Split-log, and nine other chiefs, of whom three sign their names in rude but legible manuscript; the others affix their mark only.

Is there not much reason as well as eloquence in this appeal? Apparently it was successful, as I find the Wyandots still on their land, and no question at present of the rights of the other tribes. Warrow and Split-log, two of the chiefs who sign this petition, were distinguished in the last war; they were present at the council at Fort Malden, and fought in the battle in which Tecumseh was slain.

July 18.

This evening the Thomas Jefferson arrived in the river from Buffalo, and starts early to-morrow morning for Chicago. I hastened to secure a passage as far as the island of Mackinaw; when once there, I must trust to Providence for some opportunity of going up Lake Huron to the Sault Ste. Marie to visit my friends the MacMurrays; or down the lake to the great Manitoolin Island, where the annual distribution of presents to the Indians is to take place under the auspices of the governor. If both these plans—wild plans they are, I am told—should fail, I have only to retrace my way and come down the lake, as I went up, in a steamer; but this were horridly tedious and prosaic, and I *hope* better things. So *evviva la speranza!* and Westward Ho!

"Un pezzo del cielo caduto in terra."

Mackinaw.

On a little platform not quite half-way up the wooded height which overlooks the bay, embowered in foliage, and sheltered from the tyrannous breathing of the north by the precipitous cliff, rising almost perpendicularly behind, stands the house in which I find myself at present a grateful and contented inmate. The ground in front sloping down to the shore, is laid out in a garden, with an avenue of fruit trees, the gate at the end opening on the very edge of the lake. From the porch I look down upon the scene I have endeavoured—how inadequately!—to describe to you: the little crescent bay; the village of Mackinaw; the beach thickly studded with Indian lodges; canoes, fishing, or darting hither and thither, light and buoyant as sea-birds; a tall graceful schooner swinging at anchor. Opposite rises the island of Bois-blanc, with its tufted and most luxuriant foliage. To the east we see the open lake, and in the far western distance the promontory of Michilimackinac, and the strait of that name, the portal of Lake Michigan. The exceeding beauty of this little paradise of an island, the attention which has been excited by its enchanting scenery, and the salubrity of its summer climate, the facility of communication lately afforded by the lake steamers, and its situation half-way between Detroit and the newly-settled regions of the west, are likely to render Mackinaw a sort of watering-place for the Michigan and Wisconsin fashionables, or, as the bishop expressed it, the "Rockaway of the west;" so at least it is anticipated.

How far such an accession of fashion and reputation may be desirable, I know not; I am only glad it has not yet taken place, and that I have beheld this lovely island in all its wild beauty. I am told that last year there were several strangers staying here, in spite of the want of all endurable accommodation. This year there is only one *permanent* visiter—If I may so express myself—a most agreeable little Irish-woman, with the Irish warmth of heart and ease of manner, who emigrated with her husband some years ago, and settled near St. Joseph's, in Michigan. She has brought her children here for the summer, and has her piano, her

French and Italian books, and we have begun an acquaintance which is likely to prove very pleasant.

When I left my room this morning, I remained for some time in the parlor, looking over the Wisconsin Gazette, a good sized, well-printed newspaper, published on the west shore of Lake Michigan. I was reading a most pathetic and serious address from the new settlers in Wisconsin to *the down-east girls* (*i.e.* the women of the eastern states) who are invited to go to the relief of these hapless hard-working bachelors in the backwoods. They are promised affluence and love,—the "picking and choosing among a set of the finest young fellows in the world," who were ready to fall at their feet, and make the most adoring and the most obedient of husbands! Can you fancy what a pretty thing a Wisconsin pastoral might be? Only imagine one of these despairing backwoodsmen inditing an Ovidian epistle to his unknown mistress—"*down east*,"—wooing her to come and be wooed! Well, I was enjoying this comical effusion, and thinking that women must certainly be at a premium in these parts, when suddenly the windows were darkened, and looking up, I beheld a crowd of faces, dusky, painted, wild, grotesque—with flashing eyes and white teeth, staring in upon me. I quickly threw down the paper and hastened out. The porch, the little lawn, the garden walks, were crowded with Indians, the elder chiefs and warriors sitting on the ground, or leaning silently against the pillars; the young men, women, and boys lounging and peeping about, with eager and animated looks, but all perfectly well conducted, and their voices low and pleasing to the ear. They were chiefly Ottawas and Pottowattomies, two tribes which "call brother," that is, claim relationship, and are usually in alliance, but widely different. The Ottawas are the most civilized, the Pottowattomies the least so of all the lake tribes. The Ottawa I soon distinguished by the decency of his dress, and the handkerchief knotted round the head—a custom borrowed from the early French settlers, with whom they have had much intercourse: the Pottowattomie by the more savage finery of his costume, his tall figure, and a sort of swagger in his gait. The dandyism of some of these Pottowattomie warriors is inexpressibly amusing and grotesque; I defy all Regent Street and Bond Street to go beyond them in the exhibition of self-decoration and self-complacency.

One of these exquisites, whom I distinguished as Beau Brummel, was not indeed much indedbted to a tailor, seeing he had neither a coat nor any thing else that gentlemen are accustomed to wear; but then his face was most artistically painted, the upper half of it being vermilion, with a black circle round one eye, and a white circle round the other; the lower half of a bright green, except the tip of his nose, which was also vermilion. His leggings of scarlet cloth were embroidered down the sides, and decorated with tufts of hair. The band, or garter, which confines the leggings, is always an especial bit of finery; and his were gorgeous, all embroidered with gay beads, and strings and tassels of the liveliest colours hanging down to his ankle. His moccasins were also beautifully worked with porcupine quills; he had armlets and bracelets of silver, and round his head a silver band stuck with tufts of moose-hair, died blue and red; and conspicuous above all, the eagle feather in his hair, showing he was a warrior, and had taken a scalp—*i.e.* killed his man.

Over his shoulders hung a blanket of scarlet cloth, very long and ample, which he had thrown back a little, so as to display his chest, on which a large outspread hand was painted in white. It is impossible to describe the air of perfect self-complacency with which this youth strutted about. Seeing my attention fixed upon him, he came up and shook hands with me, repeating "Bojou! bojou!"* Others immediately pressed forward also to shake hands, or rather take my hand, for they do not *shake* it; and I was soon in the midst of a crowd of perhaps thirty or forty Indians, all holding out their hands to me, or snatching mine, and repeating "bojou" with every expression of delight and good humor.

This must suffice in the way of description, for I cannot further particularize dresses; they were very various, and few so fine as my young Pottowattomie. I remember another young man, who had a common black beaver hat, all round which, in several silver bands, he had stuck a profusion of feathers, and long tufts of dyed hair, so that it formed a most gorgeous helmet. Some wore the hair hanging loose and wild in elf-locks, but others again had combed and arranged it with much care and pains.

The men seemed to engross the finery; none of the women

* This universal Indian salutation is merely a corruption of *bon jour.*

that I saw were painted. Their blankets were mostly dark blue; some had strings of beads round their necks, and silver armlets. The hair of some of the young women was very prettily aranged, being parted smooth upon the forehead, and twisted in a knot behind, very much *à la Grecque*. There is, I imagine, a very general and hearty aversion to cold water.

This morning there was a "talk" held in Mr. Schoolcraft's office, and he kindly invited me to witness the proceedings. About twenty of their principal men, including a venerable old chief, were present; the rest stood outside, crowding the doors and windows, but never attempting to enter, nor causing the slightest interruption. The old chief wore a quantity of wampum, but was otherwise undistinguished, except by his fine head and acute features. His gray hair was drawn back, and tied on the top of his head with a single feather. All, as they entered, took me by the hand with a quiet smile and a "bojou," to which I replied, as I had been instructed, "Bojou, neeje!" (Good-day, friend!) They then sat down upon the floor, all round the room. Mr. Johnston, Mrs. Schoolcraft's brother, acted as interpreter, and the business proceeded with the utmost gravity.

After some whispering among themselves, an orator of the party addressed Mr. Schoolcraft with great emphasis. Extending his hand and raising his voice, he began: "Father, I am come to tell you a piece of my mind." But when he had uttered a few sentences, Mr. Schoolcraft desired the interpreter to tell him that it was useless to speak farther on *that* subject. (I understood it to relate to some land payments.) The orator stopped immediately, and then, after a pause, he went up and took Mr. Schoolcraft's hand with a friendly air, as if to show he was not offended. Another orator then arose, and proceeded to the object of the visit, which was to ask an allowance of corn, salt, and tobacco, while they remained on the island—a request which I presume was granted, as they departed with much apparent satisfaction.

There was not a figure among them that was not a study for a painter; and how I wished that my hand had been readier with the pencil to snatch some of those picturesque heads and attitudes! But it was all so new—I was so lost in gazing, listening, observing, and trying to comprehend, that I could not make a single sketch for you, except the above, in most poor and inadequate words.

The Indians here—and fresh parties are constantly arriving—are chiefly Ottawas, from Arbre Croche, on the east of Lake Michigan; Pottowattomies; and Winnebagos, from the west of the lake; a few Menomonies and Chippewas, from the shores north-west of us;—the occasion of this assemblage being the same with all. They are on the way to the Manitoolin Islands, to receive the presents annually distributed by the British government to all those Indian tribes who were friendly to us during the wars with America, and call themselves our allies and our children, though living within the bounds of another state. Some of them make a voyage of five hundred miles to receive a few blankets and kettles; coasting along the shores, encamping at night, and paddling all day from sunrise to sunset, living on the fish or game they may meet, and the little provision they can carry with them, which consists chiefly of parched Indian corn and bear's fat. Some are out on this excursion during six weeks, or more, every year; returning to their hunting-grounds by the end of September, when the great hunting season begins, which continues through October and November; they then return to their villages and wintering-grounds. This applies generally to the tribes I find here, except the Ottawas of Arbre Croche, who have a good deal of land in cultivation, and are more stationary and civilized than the other Lake Indians. They have been for nearly a century under the care of the French jesuit missions, but do not seem to have made much advance since Henry's time, and the days when they were organised under Pontiac; they were even then considered superior in humanity and intelligence to the Chippewas and Pottowattomies, and more inclined to agriculture.

After some most sultry weather, we have had a grand storm. The wind shifted to the north-east, and rose to a hurricane. I was then sitting with my Irish friend in the mission-house; and while the little bay lay almost tranquil, gleam and shadow floating over its bosom, the expanse of the main lake was like the ocean lashed to fury. On the east side of the island the billows came "rolling with might," flinging themselves in wrath and foam far up the land. It was a magnificent spectacle. Returning home, I was anxious to see how the wigwam establishments had stood out the storm, and was surprised to find that little or no damage had been done. I peeped into several, with a nod and a *bojou*, and found the inmates very snug. Here and there a mat was blown away, but none of the poles were displaced or blown down, which I had firmly expected.

Though all these lodges seem nearly alike to a casual observer, I was soon aware of differences and gradations in the particular arrangements, which are amusingly characteristic of the various inhabitants. There is one lodge, a little to the east of us, which I call the Chateau. It is rather larger and loftier than the others: the mats which cover it are whiter and of a neater texture than usual. The blanket which hangs before the opening is new and clean. The inmates, ten in number, are well and handsomely dressed; even the women and children have abundance of ornaments; and as for the gay cradle of the baby, I quite covet it—it is so gorgeously elegant. I supposed at first that this must be the lodge of a chief; but I have since understood that the chief is seldom either so well lodged or so well dressed as the others, it being a part of his policy to avoid everything like ostentation, or rather to be ostentatiously poor and plain in his apparel and possessions. This wigwam belongs to an Ottawa, remarkable for his skill in hunting, and for his habitual abstinence from the "fire-water." He is a baptized Roman Catholic, belonging to the mission at Arbre Croche, and is reputed a rich man.

Not far from this, and almost immediately in front of our house, stands another wigwam, a most wretched concern. The owners have not mats enough to screen them from the weather; and the bare poles are exposed through the "looped and windowed raggedness" on every side. The woman, with her long neglected hair, is always seen cowering despondingly over the embers of her fire, as if lost in sad reveries. Two naked children are scrambling among the pebbles on the shore. The man wrapt in a dirty ragged blanket, without a single ornament, looks the image of savage inebriety and ferocity. Observe that these are the two extremes, and that between them are many gradations of comfort, order, and respectability. An Indian is *respectable* in his own community, in proportion as his wife and children look fat and well fed; this being a proof of his prowess and success as a hunter, and his consequent riches.

I was loitering by the garden gate this evening, about sunset, looking at the beautiful effects which the storm of the morning had left in the sky and on the lake. I heard the sound of the Indian drum mingled with the shouts and yells and shrieks of the intoxicated savages, who were drinking in front of the village whiskey-store;—when at this moment a man came slowly up, whom I recognized as one of the Ottawa chiefs, who had often attracted my attention. His name is Kim,e,wun, which signifies the Rain, or rather "it rains." He now stood before me, one of the noblest figures I ever beheld, above six feet high, erect as a forest pine. A red and green handkerchief was twined round his head with much elegance, and knotted in front, with the two ends projecting; his black hair fell from beneath it, and his small black piercing eyes glittered from among its masses, like stars glancing through the thunder clouds. His ample blanket was thrown over his left shoulder, and brought under his right arm, so as to leave it free and exposed; and a sculptor might have envied the disposition of the whole drapery—it was so felicitous, so richly graceful.* He stood in a contemplative attitude, evidently undecided whether he should join his drunken companions in their night revel, or return, like a wise man, to his lodge and his mat. He advanced a few steps, then turned, then paused and listened—then turned back again. I retired a little within the gate, to watch, unseen, the issue of the conflict. Alas! it was soon decided—the fatal temptation prevailed over better thoughts. He suddenly drew his blanket round him, and strided onwards in the direction of the village, treading the earth with an air of

* While among the Indians, I often had occasion to observe that what we call the *antique* and the *ideal* are merely free, unstudied nature. Since my return from Canada, I have seen some sketches made by Mr. Harvey when in Ireland—figures of the Cork and Kerry girls, folded in their large blue cloaks; and I remember, on opening the book, I took them for drawings after the antique—figures brought from Herculaneum or Pompeii, or some newly-discovered Greek temple.

defiance, and a step which would have become a prince.

On returning home, I mentioned this scene to Mr. and Mrs. Schoolcraft, as I do everything which strikes me, that I may profit by their remarks and explanations. Mr. S. told me a laughable anecdote.

A distinguished Pottowattomie presented himself to the Indian agent at Chicago, and observing that he was a very good man, very good indeed—and a good friend to the Long-Knives (the Americans), requested a dram of whiskey. The agent replied, that he never gave whiskey to *good* men,—*good* men never asked for whiskey; and never drink it. It was only *bad* Indians who asked for whiskey, or liked to drink it. "Then," replied the Indian in his broken English, "me damn rascal!"

The revel continued far through the night, for I heard the wild yelling and whooping of the savages long after I had gone to rest. I can now conceive what it must be to hear that shrill prolonged cry (unlike any sound I ever heard in my life before) in the solitude of the forest, and when it is the certain harbinger of death.

It is surprising to me, considering the number of savages congregated together, and the excess of drunkenness, that no mischief is done; that there has been no fighting, no robberies committed, and that there is a feeling of perfect security around me.

The women, they tell me, have taken away their husband's knives and tomahawks, and hidden them—wisely enough. At this time there are about twelve hundred Indians here. The fort is empty—the garrison having been withdrawn as useless; and perhaps there are not a hundred white men in the island,—rather unequal odds! And then that fearful Michilimackinac in full view, with all its horrid murderous associations!* But do not for a moment imagine that I feel

* Michilimackinac was one of the forts surprised by the Indians at the breaking out of the Pontiac war, when seventy British soldiers with their officers were murdered and scalped. Henry gives a most vivid description of this scene of horror in few words. He was present, and escaped through the friendship of an Indian (Wa,wa,tam), who, in consequence of a dream in early youth, had adopted him as his brother.

fear, or the slightest doubt of security; only a sort of thrill which enhances the enjoyment I have in these wild scenes—a thrill such as one feels in the presence of danger when most safe from it—such as I felt when bending over the rapids of Niagara.

The Indians, apparently, have no idea of correcting or restraining their children; personal chastisement is unheard of. They say that before a child has any understanding there is no use in correcting it; and when old enough to understand, no one has a right to correct it. Thus the fixed, inherent sentiment of personal independence grows up with the Indians from earliest infancy. The will of an Indian child is not forced; he has nothing to learn but what he sees done around him, and he learns by imitation. I hear no scolding, no tones of command or reproof; but I see no evil results from this mild system, for the general reverence and affection of children for parents is delightful: where there is no obedience exacted, there can be no rebellion; they dream not of either, and all live in peace under the same wigwam.

I observe, while loitering among them, that they seldom raise their voices, and they pronounce several words much more softly than we write them. Wigwam, a house, they pronounce *wee-ga-waum;* moccasin, a shoe, *muck-a-zeen;* manito, spirit, *mo-needo,*—lengthening the vowels, and softening the aspirates. *Chippewa* is properly *O,jib,wày; ab,bin,-no,jee* is a little child. The accent of the women is particularly soft, with a sort of plaintive modulation, reminding me of recitative. Their low laugh is quite musical, and has something infantine in it. I sometimes hear them sing, and the strain is generally in a minor key; but I cannot succeed in detecting or retaining an entire or distinct tune. I am, however, bent on bringing you an Indian song, if I can catch one.

July 29.

Where was I? Where did I leave off four days ago? O—at Mackinaw! that fairy island, which I shall never see again! and which I should have dearly liked to filch from the Americans, and carry home to you in my dressing-box, or, *perdie*, in my tooth-pick case—but, good lack! to see the ups and downs of this (new) world! I take up my tale a hundred miles from it—but before I tell you where I am now, I must take you over the ground, or rather over the water, in a proper and journal-like style.

I was sitting last Friday, at sultry noon-tide, under the shadow of a schooner which had just anchored alongside the little pier—sketching and dreaming—when up came a messenger, breathless, to say that a boat was going off for the Sault Ste. Marie, in which I could be accommodated with a passage. Now this was precisely what I had been wishing and waiting for, and yet I heard the information with an emotion of regret. I had become every day more attached to the society of Mrs. Schoolcraft—more interested about her; and the idea of parting, and parting suddenly, took me by surprise, and was anything but agreeable. On reaching the house, I found all in movement, and learned, to my inexpressible delight, that my friend would take the opportunity of paying a visit to her mother and family, and, with her children, was to accompany me on my voyage.

We had but one hour to prepare packages, provisions, everything—and in one hour all was ready.

This voyage of two days was to be made in a little Canadian bateau, rowed by five *voyageurs* from the Sault. The boat might have carried fifteen persons, hardly more, and was rather clumsy in form. The two ends were appropriated to the rowers, baggage, and provisions; in the centre there was a clear space, with a locker on each side, on which we sat or reclined, having stowed away in them our smaller and more valuable packages. This was the internal arrangement.

The distance to the Sault, or, as the Americans call it, the *Sou*, is not more than thirty miles over land, as the bird flies; but the whole region being one mass of tangled forest and swamp, infested with bears and mosquitoes, it is seldom crossed but in winter, and in snow shoes. The usual route by water is ninety-four miles.

At three o'clock in the afternoon, with a favourable breeze, we launched forth on the lake, and having rowed about a mile from the shore, the little square sail was hoisted, and away we went merrily over the blue waves.

For a detailed account of the *voyageurs*, or Canadian boatmen, their peculiar condition and mode of life, I refer you to Washington Irving's "Astoria;" what he describes them to *have been*, and what Henry represents them in his time, they are even now, in these regions of the upper lakes.* But the voyageurs in our boat were not favourable specimens of their very amusing and peculiar class. They were fatigued after rowing for three days previous, and had only two helpless women to deal with. As soon, therefore, as the sail was hoisted, two began to play cards on the top of a keg, the other two went to sleep. The youngest and most intelligent of the set, a lively, half-breed boy of eighteen, took the helm. He told us with great self-complacency that he was *captain*, and that it was already the third time that he had been elected by his comrades to this dignity—but I cannot say he had a very obedient crew.

About seven o'clock we landed to cook our supper on an island which is commemorated by Henry as the Isles des

* As I shall have much to say hereafter of this peculiar class of people, to save both reader and author time and trouble, the passage is here given.

"The voyageurs form a kind of confraternity in the Canadas, like the arrieros or carriers of Spain. The dress of these people is generally half civilized, half savage. They wear a capote or surcoat, made of a blanket, a striped cotton shirt, cloth trowsers or leathern leggings, moccasins of deer skin, and a belt of variegated worsted, from which are suspended the knife, tobacco-pouch, and other articles. Their language is of the same piebald character, being a French patois embroidered with English and Italian words and phrases. They are generally of French descent, and inherit much of the gaiety and lightness of heart of their ancestors; they inherit, too, a fund of civility and complaisance, and instead of that hardness and grossness, which men in laborious life are apt to indulge towards each other, they are mutually obliging and accommodating, interchanging kind offices, yielding each other assistance and comfort in every emergency, and using the familiar appellations of *cousin* and *brother*, when there is in fact no relationship. No men are more submissive to their leaders and employers, more capable of enduring hardships, or more good-humoured under privations. Never are they so happy as when on long and rough expeditions, towing up rivers or coasting lakes. They are dexterous boat-men, vigorous and adroit with the oar or paddle, and will row from morning till night without a murmur. The steersman often sings an old French song, with some regular burthen, in which they all join, keeping time with their oars. If at any time they flag in spirits or relax in exertion, it is but necessary to strike up a song of this kind to put them all in fresh spirits and activity."—*Astoria*, vol. i. chap. 4.

Outardes, and is now Goose Island. Mrs. Schoolcraft undertook the general management with all the alertness of one accustomed to these *impromptu* arrangements, and I did my best in my new avocation—dragged one or two blasted boughs to the fire—the least of them twice as big as myself—and laid the cloth upon the pebbly beach. The enormous fire was to keep off the mosquitoes, in which we succeeded pretty well, swallowing, however, as much smoke as would have dried us externally into hams or red herrings. We then returned to the boat, spread a bed for the children, (who were my delight,) in the bottom of it, with mats and blankets, and disposed our own, on the lockers on each side, with buffalo skins, blankets, shawls, cloaks, and whatever was available, with my writing-case for a pillow.

After sunset the breeze fell: the men were urged to row, but pleaded fatigue, and that they were hired for the day, and not for the night, (which is the custom.) One by one they sulkily abandoned their oars, and sunk to sleep under their blankets, all but our young captain; like Ulysses, when steering away from Calypso—

> Placed at the helm he sat, and watched the skies,
> Nor closed in sleep his ever-watchful eyes.

He kept himself awake by singing hymns, in which Mrs. Schoolcraft joined him. I lay still, looking at the stars and listening: when there was a pause in the singing, we kept up the conversation, fearing lest sleep should overcome our only pilot and guardian. Thus we floated on beneath that divine canopy—"which love had spread to curtain the sleeping world:" it was a most lovely and blessed night, bright and calm and warm, and we made some little way, for both wind and current were in our favour.

As we were coasting a little shadowy island, our captain mentioned a strange circumstance, very illustrative of Indian life and character. A short time ago a young Chippewa hunter, whom he knew, was shooting squirrels on this spot, when by some chance a large blighted pine fell upon him, knocking him down and crushing his leg, which was fractured in two places. He could not rise, he could not remove the tree which was lying across his broken leg. He was in a little uninhabited island, without the slightest probability of passing aid, and to lie there and starve to death in agonies, seemed all that was left to him. In this dilemma, with all the fortitude and promptitude of resource of a thorough-bred Indian, he took out his knife, cut off his own leg, bound it up, dragged himself along the ground to his hunting canoe, and paddled himself home to his wigwam on a distant island, where the cure of his wound was completed. The man is still alive.

Perhaps this story appears to you incredible. I believe it firmly; at the time, and since then, I heard other instances of Indian fortitude, and of their courage and skill in performing some of the boldest and most critical operations in surgery, which I really cannot venture to set down. *You* would believe them if I could swear that I had witnessed them with "my own two good-looking eyes," not otherwise. But I will mention one or two of the least marvellous of these stories. There was a young chief and famous hunter, whose arm was shattered by the bursting of his rifle. No one would venture the amputation, and it was bound up with certain herbs and dressings, accompanied with many magical ceremonies. The young man, who seemed aware of the inefficacy of such expedients, waited till the moment when he should be left alone. He had mean time, with pain and difficulty, hacked one of his knives into a saw; with this he completed the amputation of his own arm; and when his relations appeared, they found the arm lying at one end of the wigwam, and the patient sitting at the other, with his wound bound up, and smoking with great tranquillity.

Mrs. Schoolcraft told me of a young Chippewa who went on a hunting expedition with his wife only; they were encamped at a considerable distance from the village, when the woman was seized with the pains of child-birth. This is in general a very easy matter among the Indian women, cases of danger or death being exceedingly rare; but on this occasion some unusual and horrible difficulty occurred. The husband, who was described to me as an affectionate, gentle spirited man, much attached to his wife, did his best to assist her; but after a few struggles she became insensible, and lay, as he supposed, dead. He took out his knife, and with astonishing presence of mind, performed on his wife the Cesarean operation, saved his infant, and ultimately the mother, and brought them both home on a sleigh to his village at the

Sault, where, as Mrs. Schoolcraft told me, she had frequently seen both the man and woman.

* * * *

We remained in conversation till long after midnight; then the boat was moored to a tree, but kept off shore, for fear of the mosquitoes, and we addressed ourselves to sleep. I remember lying awake for some minutes, looking up at the quiet stars, and around upon the dark weltering waters, and at the faint waning moon, just suspended on the very edge of the horizon. I saw it sink—sink into the bosom of the lake, as if to rest, and then with a thought of far-off friends, and a most fervent thanksgiving. I dropped asleep. It is odd that I did not think of praying for protection, and that no sense of fear came over me; it seemed as if the eye of God himself looked down upon me; that I *was* protected. I do not say I *thought* this any more than the unweaned child in its cradle; but I had some such feeling of unconscious trust and love, now I recall those moments.

I slept, however, uneasily, not being yet accustomed to a board and a blanket; *ça viendra avec le temps*. About dawn I awoke in a sort of stupor, but after bathing my face and hands over the boat side, I felt refreshed. The voyageurs, after a good night's rest, were in better humour, and took manfully to their oars. Soon after sunrise, we passed round that very conspicuous cape, famous in the history of north-west adventurers, called the "Grand Détour," half-way between Mackinaw and the Sault. Now, if you look at the map, you will see that our course was henceforth quite altered; we had been running down the coast of the main land towards the east; we had now to turn short round the point, and steer almost due west; hence its most fitting name, the Grand Détour. The wind, hitherto favourable, was now dead against us. This part of Lake Huron is studded with little islands, which, as well as the neighbouring main land, are all uninhabited, yet clothed with the richest, loveliest, most fantastic vegetation, and no doubt swarming with animal life.

I cannot, I dare not, attempt to describe to you the strange sensation one has, thus thrown for a time beyond the bounds of civilized humanity, or indeed any humanity; nor the wild yet solemn reveries which come over one in the midst of this wilderness of woods and waters. All was so solitary, so grand in its solitude, as if nature unviolated sufficed to herself. Two days and nights the solitude was unbroken; not a trace of social life, not a human being, not a canoe, not even a deserted wigwam, met our view. Our little boat held on its way over the placid lake and among green tufted islands; and we its inmates, two women, differing in clime, nation, complexion, strangers to each other but a few days ago, might have fancied ourselves alone in a new-born world.

We landed to boil our kettle, and breakfast on a point of the island of St. Joseph's. This most beautiful island is between thirty and forty miles in length, and nearly a hundred miles in circumference, and towards the centre the land is high and picturesque. They tell me that on the other side of the island there is a settlement of whites and Indians. Another large island, Drummond's Isle, was for a short time in view. We had also a settlement here, but it was unaccountably surrendered to the Americans. If now you look at the map, you will wonder, as I did, that in retaining St. Joseph's and the Manitoolin islands, we gave up Drummond's island. Both these islands had forts and garrisons during the war.

By the time breakfast was over, the children had gathered some fine strawberries; the heat had now become almost intolerable, and unluckily we had no awning. The men rowed languidly, and we made but little way; we coasted along the south shore of St. Joseph's, through fields of rushes, miles in extent, across Lake George, and Muddy Lake; (the name, I thought, must be a libel, for it was as clear as a crystal and as blue as heaven; but they say that, like a sulky temper, the least ruffle of wind turns it as black as ditchwater, and it does not subside again in a hurry,) and then came a succession of openings spotted with lovely islands, all solitary. The sky was without a cloud, a speck—except when the great fish-eagle was descried sailing over its blue depths—the water without a wave. We were too hot and too languid to converse. Nothing disturbed the deep noon-tide stillness, but the dip of the oars, or the spring and splash of a sturgeon as he leapt from the surface of the lake, leaving a circle of little wavelets spreading around. All the islands we passed were so woody, and so infested with mosquitoes, that we could not land and light our fire, till we reached the entrance of

St. Mary's River, between Nebish island and the main land.

Here was a well-known spot, a sort of little opening on a flat shore, called the *Encampment*, because a party of boatmen coming down from Lake Superior, and camping here for the night, were surprised by the frost, and obliged to remain the whole winter till the opening of the ice in the spring. After rowing all this hot day till seven o'clock against the wind, (what there was of it,) and against the current coming rapidly and strongly down from Lake Superior, we did at length reach this promised harbour of rest and refreshment. Alas! there was neither for us; the moment our boat touched the shore, we were enveloped in a cloud of mosquitoes. Fires were lighted instantly, six were burning in a circle at once; we were well nigh suffocated and smoke-dried —all in vain. At last we left the voyageurs to boil the kettle, and retreated to our boat, desiring them to make us fast to a tree by a long rope; then, each of us taking an oar—I only wish you could have seen us—we pushed off from the land, while the children were sweeping away the enemy with green boughs. This being done, we commenced supper, really half famished, and were too much engrossed to look about us. Suddenly we were again surrounded by our adversaries; they came upon us in swarms, in clouds, in myriads, entering our eyes, our noses, our mouths, stinging till the blood followed. We had, unawares, and while absorbed in our culinary operations, drifted into the shore, got entangled among the roots of trees, and were with difficulty extricated, presenting all the time a fair mark and a rich banquet for our detested tormentors. The dear children cried with agony and impatience, and but for shame I could almost have cried too.

I had suffered from these plagues in Italy; you too, by this time, may probably know what they are in the southern countries of the old world; but 'tis a jest, believe me, to encountering a forest full of them in these wild regions. I had heard much, and much was I forewarned, but never could have conceived the torture they can inflict, nor the impossibility of escape, defence, or endurance. Some amiable person, who took an especial interest in our future welfare, in enumerating the torments prepared for hardened sinners, assures us that they will be stung by mosquitoes all made of brass, and as large as black beetles—he was an ignoramus and a bungler; you may credit me, that the brass is quite an unnecessary improvement, and the increase of size equally superfluous. Mosquitoes, as they exist in this upper world, are as pretty and perfect a plague as the most ingenious amateur sinner-tormentor ever devised. Observe, that a mosquito does not sting like a wasp, or a gad-fly; he has a long proboscis like an awl, with which he bores your veins, and pumps the life-blood out of you, leaving venom and fever behind. Enough of mosquitoes—I will never again do more than allude to them; only they are enough to make Philosophy go hang herself, and Patience swear like a Turk or a trooper.

Well, we left this most detestable and inhospitable shore as soon as possible, but the enemy followed us and we did not soon get rid of them; night came on, and we were still twenty miles below the Sault.

I offered an extra gratuity to the men, if they would keep to their oars without interuption; and then, fairly exhausted, lay down on my locker and blanket. But whenever I woke from uneasy, restless slumbers, *there* was Mrs. Schoolcraft, bending over her sleeping children, and waving off the mosquitoes, singing all the time a low, melancholy Indian song; while the northern lights were streaming and dancing in the sky, and the fitful moaning of the wind, the gathering clouds, and chilly atmosphere, foretold a change of weather. This would have been the *comble de malheur*. When daylight came, we passed Sugar Island, where immense quantities of maple sugar are made every spring, and just as the rain began to fall in earnest, we arrived at the Sault Ste. Marie. On one side of the river, Mrs. Schoolcraft was welcomed by her mother; and on the other, my friends, the MacMurrays, received me with delighted and delightful hospitality. I went to bed—oh! the luxury!—and slept for six hours.

One of the gratifications I had anticipated in coming hither—my strongest inducement perhaps—was an introduction to the mother of my two friends, of whom her children so delighted to speak, and of whom I had heard much from other sources. A woman of pure Indian blood, of a race celebrated in these regions as warriors and chiefs from generation to generation, who had never resided within the pale of what we call civilized life, whose habits and manners were those of a genuine Indian squaw, and whose talents and domestic virtues commanded the highest respect, was, as you may suppose, an object of the deepest interest to me. I observed that not only her own children, but her two sons-in-law, Mr. MacMurray and Mr. Schoolcraft, both educated in good society, the one a clergyman and the other a man of science and literature, looked up to this remarkable woman with sentiments of affection and veneration.

As soon, then, as I was a little refreshed after my two nights on the lake, and my battles with the mosquitoes, we paddled over the river to dine with Mrs. Johnston: she resides in a large log-house close upon the shore; there is a little portico in front with seats, and the interior is most comfortable. The old lady herself is rather large in person, with the strongest marked Indian features, a countenance, open, benevolent, and intelligent, and a maner perfectly easy—simple, yet with something of motherly dignity, becoming the head of her large family. She received me most affectionately, and we entered into conversation—Mrs. Schoolcraft, who looked all animation and happiness, acting as interpreter. Mrs. Johnston speaks no English, but can understand it a little, and the Canadian French still better; but in her own language she is eloquent, and her voice, like that of her people, low and musical; many kind words were exchanged, and when I said anything that pleased her, she laughed softly like a child.—I was not well, and much fevered, and I remember she took me in her arms, laid me down on a couch, and began to rub my feet, soothing and caressing me. She called me Nindannis, daughter, and I called her Neengai, mother, (though how different from my own fair mother, I thought, as I looked up gratefully in her dark Indian face!) She set before us the best dressed and best served dinner I had seen since I left Toronto, and presided at her table, and did the honours of her house with unembarrassed, unaffected propriety. My attempts to speak Indian, caused, of course, considerable amusement; if I do not make progress, it will not be for want of teaching and teachers.

After dinner we took a walk to visit Mrs. Johnston's brother, Wayish,ky, whose wigwam is at a little distance, on the verge of the burial-ground. The lodge is of genuine Chippewa form, like an egg cut in half lengthways. It is

 Wayish,ky

formed of poles stuck in the ground, and bent over at top, strengthened with a few wattles and boards; the whole is covered over with mats, birch-bark, and skins; a large blanket formed the door or curtain, which was not ungracefully looped aside. Wayish,ky, being a great man, has also a smaller lodge hard by, which serves as a storehouse and kitchen.

Rude as was the exterior of Wayish,ky's hut, the interior presented every appearance of comfort, and even *elegance*, according to the Indian notions of both. It formed a good-sized room: a raised couch ran all round like a Turkish divan, serving both for seats and beds, and covered with very soft and beautiful matting of various colours and patterns. The chests and baskets of birch-bark, containing the family wardrobe and property; the rifles, the hunting and fishing tackle, were stowed away all round very tidily; I observed a coffee-mill nailed up to one of the posts or stakes; the floor was trodden down hard and perfectly clean, and there was a place for a fire in the middle: there was no window, but quite sufficient light and air were admitted through the door, and through an aperture in the roof. There was no disagreeable smell, and everything looked neat and clean. We found Wayish,ky and his wife and three of their children seated in the lodge, and as it was Sunday, and they are all Christians, no work was going forward. They received me with genuine and simple politeness, each taking my hand with a gentle inclination of the head, and some words of welcome murmured in their own soft language. We then sat down.

The conversation became very lively; and, if I might judge from looks and tones, very affectionate. I *sported* my last new words and phrases with great effect, and when I had exhausted my vocabulary—which was very soon—I amused myself with looking and listening.

Mrs. Wayish,ky (I forget her proper name) must have been a very beautiful woman. Though now no longer young, and the mother of twelve children, she is one of the handsomest Indian women I have yet seen. The number of her children is remarkable, for in general there are few large families among the Indians. Her daughter Zah,gah,see,ga,-quay, (*the sunbeams breaking through a cloud,*) is a very beautiful girl, with eyes that are a warrant for her poetical name—she is about sixteen. Wayish,ky himself is a grave, dignified man about fifty. He told me that his eldest son had gone down to the Manitoolin Island to represent his family, and receive his quota of presents. His youngest son he had sent to a college in the United States, to be educated in the learning of the white men. Mrs. Schoolcraft whispered me that this poor boy is now dying of consumption, owing to the confinement and change of living, and that the parents knew it. Wayish,ky seemed aware that we were alluding to his son, for his eye at that moment rested on me, and such an expression of keen pain came suddenly over his fine countenance, it was as if a knife had struck him, and I really felt it in my heart, and see it still before me—that look of misery.

After about an hour we left this good and interesting family. I lingered for a while on the burial-ground, looking over the rapids, and watching with a mixture of admiration and terror several little canoes which were fishing in the midst of the boiling surge, dancing and popping about like corks. The canoe used for fishing is very small and light; one man (or woman more commonly) sits in the stern, and steers with a paddle; the fisher places himself upright on the prow, balancing a long pole with both hands, at the end of which is a scoop-net. This he every minute dips into the water, bringing up at each dip a fish, and sometimes two. I used to admire the fishermen on the Arno, and those on the Lagune, and above all the Neapolitan fishermen, hauling in their nets, or diving like ducks, but I never saw anything like these Indians. The manner in which they keep their position upon a footing of a few inches, is to me as incomprehensible as the beauty of their forms and attitudes, swayed by every movement and turn of their dancing, fragile barks, is admirable.

George Johnston, on whose arm I was leaning, (and I had much ado to *reach* it,) gave me such a vivid idea of the delight of coming down the cataract in a canoe, that I am half resolved to attempt it. Terrific as it appears, yet in a good canoe, and with experienced guides, there is no absolute danger, and it must be a glorious sensation.

Mr. Johnston had spent the last fall and winter in the country, beyond Lake Superior, towards the forks of the Mississippi, where he had been employed as American agent to arrange the boundary line between the country of the Chippewas and that of their neigbours and implacable enemies, the Sioux. His mediation appeared successful for the time, and he smoked the pipe of peace with both tribes; but during the spring this ferocious war has again broken out, and he seems to think that nothing but the annihilation of either one nation or the other will entirely put an end to their conflicts; "for there is no point at which the Indian law of retaliation stops, short of the extermination of one of the parties."

I asked him how it is that in their wars the Indians make no distinction between the warriors opposed to them and helpless women and children?—how it could be with a brave and manly people, that the scalps taken from the weak, the helpless, the unresisting, were as honourable as those torn from the warrior's skull? And I described to him the horror which this custom inspired—this, which of all their customs, most justifies the name of *savage!*

He said it was inseparable from their principles of war and their mode of warfare; the first consists in inflicting the greatest possible insult and injury on their foe with the least possible risk to themselves. This truly savage law of honour we might call cowardly, but that, being associated with the bravest contempt of danger and pain, it seems nearer to the natural law. With regard to the mode of warfare, they have rarely pitched battles, but skirmishes, surprises, ambuscades, and sudden forays into each other's hunting-grounds and villages. The usual practice is to creep stealthily on the enemy's village or hunting-encampment, and wait till just after the dawn; then, at the moment the sleepers in the lodges are rising, the ambushed warriors stoop and level their pieces about two feet from the ground, which thus slaughter indiscriminately. If they find one of the enemy's lodges undefended, they murder its inmates, that when the owner returns he may find his hearth desolate; for this is exquisite vengeance! But outrage against the chastity of women is absolutely unknown under any degree of furious excitement.*

* "The whole history of Indian warfare," says Mr. Schoolcraft, "might be challenged in vain for a solitary instance of this kind. The Indians believe that to take a dishonourable advantage of their female prisoners, would destroy their luck in hunting; it would be considered as effeminate and degrading in a warrior, and render him unfit for, and unworthy of, all manly achievement."

The respect of female honour will remind you of the ancient Germans, as described by Julius Cæsar: he contrasts in some surprise their forbearance with the very opposite conduct of the Romans; and even down to this present day, if I recollect rightly, the history of our European wars and sieges will bear out this early and characteristic distinction between the Latin and Teutonic nations. Am I right, or am I not?

To return to the Indians. After telling me some other particulars, which gave me a clearer view of their notions and feelings on these points than I ever had before, my informant mildly added,—"It is a constant and favourite subject of reproach against the Indians—this barbarism of their desultory warfare; but I should think more women and children have perished in *one* of your civilized sieges, and that in late times, than during the whole war between the Chippewas and Sioux, and *that* has lasted a century."

I was silent, for there is a sensible proverb about taking care of our own glass windows: and I wonder if any of the recorded atrocities of Indian warfare or Indian vengeance, or all of them together, ever exceeded Massena's retreat from Portugal,—and the French call themselves civilized. A war party of Indians, perhaps two or three hundred, (and that is a very large number,) dance their war dance, go out and burn a village, and bring back twenty or thirty scalps. *They* are savages and heathens. We Europeans fight a battle, leave fifty thousand dead or dying by inches on the field, and a hundred thousand to mourn them, desolate; but *we* are civilized and Christians. Then only look into the motives and causes of our bloodiest European wars as revealed in the private history of courts:—the miserable, puerile, degrading intrigues which set man against man—so horridly disproportioned to the horrid result! and then see the Indian take up his war-hatchet in vengeance for some personal injury, or from motives that rouse all the natural feelings of the natural man within him! Really I do not see that an Indian warrior, flourishing his tomahawk, and smeared with his enemy's blood, is so very much a greater savage that the pipe-clayed, padded, embroidered personage, who, without cause or motive, has sold himself to slay or be slain: one scalps his enemy, the other rips him open with a sabre; one smashes his brains with a tomahawk, and the other blows him to atoms with a cannon-ball: and to me, femininely speaking, there is not a needle's point difference between the one and the other. If war be unchristian and barbarous, then war as a *science* is more absurd, unnatural, unchristian, than war as a *passion*.

This, perhaps, is putting it all too strongly, and a little exaggerated—

God forbid that I should think to disparage the blessings of civilization! I am a woman, and to the progress of civilization alone can we women look for release from many pains and penalties and liabilities, which now lie heavily upon us. Neither am I greatly in love with savage life, with all its picturesque accompaniments and lofty virtues. I see no reason why these virtues should be necessarily connected with dirt, ignorance, and barbarism. I am thankful to live in a land of literature and steam-engines. Chatsworth is better than a wigwam, and a seventy-four is a finer thing than a bark canoe. I do not *positively* assert that Taglioni dances more gracefully than the Little-Pure tobacco-smoker, nor that soap and water are preferable as cosmetics to tallow and charcoal; for these are matters of taste, and mine may be disputed. But I do say, that if our advantages of intellect and refinement are not to lead on to farther moral superiority, I prefer the Indians on the score of consistency; they are what they profess to be, and we are *not* what we profess to be. They profess to be warriors and hunters, and are so; we profess to be Christians, and civilized—are we so?

Then as to the mere point of cruelty;—there is something to be said on this point too. Ferocity, when the hot blood is up, and all the demon in man is roused by every conceivable excitement, I can understand better than the Indian can comprehend the tender mercies of our law. Owyawatta, better known by his English name, Red-Jacket, was once seen hurrying from the town of Buffalo, with rapid strides, and every mark of disgust and consternation in his face. Three malefactors were to be hung that morning, and the Indian warrior had not nerve to face the horrid spectacle, although

> "In sober truth the veriest devil
> That ere clenched fingers in a captive's hair.'

Thus endeth my homily for to-night.

* * * *

The more I looked upon those glancing, dancing rapids, the more resolute I grew to venture myself in the midst of them. George Johnston went to seek a fit canoe and a dexterous steersman, and meantime I strolled away to pay a visit to Wayish,ky's family, and made a sketch of their lodge, while pretty Zah,gah,see,gah,qua held the umbrella to shade me.

The canoe being ready, I went up to the top of the portage, and we launched into the river. It was a small fishing canoe about ten feet long, quite new, and light and elegant and buoyant as a bird on the waters. I reclined on a mat at the bottom, Indian fashion, (there are no seats in a genuine Indian canoe;) in a minute we were within the verge of the rapids, and down we went with a whirl and a splash! —the white surge leaping around me—over me. The Indian with astonishing dexterity kept the head of the canoe to the breakers, and somehow or other we danced through them. I could see, as I looked over the edge of the canoe, that the passage between the rocks was sometimes not more than two feet in width, and we had to turn sharp angles—a touch of which would have sent us to destruction—all this I could see through the transparent eddying waters, but I can truly say, I had not even a momentary sensation of fear, but rather of giddy, breathless, delicious excitement. I could even admire the beautiful attitude of a fisher, past whom we swept as we came to the bottom. The whole affair, from the moment in entered the canoe till I reached the landing place, occupied seven minutes, and the distance is about three quarters of a mile.*

My Indians were enchanted, and when I reached *home,* my good friends were not less delighted at my exploit: they told me I was the first European female who had ever performed it, and assuredly I shall not be the last. I recommend it as an exercise before breakfast. Two glasses of champagne could not have made me more tipsy and more self-com-

* "The total descent of the Fall of St. Mary's has been ascertained to be twenty-two and a half perpendicular feet. It has been found impracticable to ascend the rapid; but canoes have ventured down, though the experiment is extremely nervous and hazardous, and avoided by a portage, two miles long, which connects the navigable parts of the strait." —*Bouchette's Canada.*

placent! As for my Neengai, she laughed, clapped her hands, and embraced me several times. I was declared duly initiated, and adopted into the family by the name of Wah,sah,ge,wah,no,qua. They had already called me among themselves, in reference to my complexion and my travelling propensities. O,daw,yaun,gee, *the fair changing moon*, or rather, *the fair moon which changes her place*; but now, in compliment to my successful achievement, Mrs. Johnston bestowed this new appellation, which I much prefer. It signifies *the bright foam*, or more properly, with the feminine adjunct *qua*, *the woman of the bright foam*; and by this name I am henceforth to be known among the Chippewas.

July 31.

This last evening of my sojourn at the Sault Ste. Marie is very melancholy—we have been all very sad. Mr. and Mrs. MacMurray are to accompany me in my voyage down the lake to the Manitoolin Islands, having some business to transact with the governor:—so you see Providence *does* take care of me! how I could have got there alone, I cannot tell, but I must have tried. At first we had arranged to go in a bark canoe; the very canoe which belonged to Captain Back, and which is now lying in Mr. MacMurray's court-yard; but our party will be large, and we shall be encumbered with much baggage and provisions—not having yet learned to live on the portable maize and fat: our voyage is likely to take three days and a half, even if the weather continues favourable, and if it do not, why we shall be obliged to put into some creek or harbour, and pitch our tent, gipsy fashion, for a day or two. There is not a settlement nor a habitation on our route, nothing but lake and forest. The distance is about one hundred and seventy miles, rather more than less; Mr. MacMurray therefore advises a bateau, in which, if we do not get on so quickly, we shall have more space and comfort—and thus it is to be.

I am sorry to leave these kind, excellent people, but most I regret Mrs. Schoolcraft.

* * * *

August 1.

The morning of our departure rose bright and beautiful, and the loading and arranging our little boat was a scene of great animation. I thought I had said all my adieus the night before, but at early dawn my good Neengai came paddling across the river with various kind offerings for her daughter Wa,sah,ge,wo,no,qua, which she thought might be pleasant or useful, and more *last* affectionate words from Mrs. Schoolcraft. We then exchanged a long farewell embrace, and she turned away with tears, got into her little canoe, which could scarcely contain two persons, and handling her paddle with singular grace and dexterity, shot over the blue water, without venturing once to look back! I leaned over the side of our boat, and strained my eyes to catch a last glimpse of the white spray of the rapids, and her little canoe skimming over the expanse between, like a black dot; and this was the last I saw of my dear good Chippewa mamma!

Meantime we were proceeding rapidly down the beautiful river, and through its winding channels. Our party consisted of Mr. and Mrs. MacMurray and their lovely boy, myself, and the two Indian girls—my cousin Zah,gah,see,ga,qua, and Angelique, the child's attendant.

These two girls were, for Indians, singularly beautiful; they would have been beautiful anywhere. Angelique, though of unmixed Indian blood, has a face of the most perfect oval, a clear brown complexion, the long, half-shaded eye, which the French call *coupé en amande;* the nose slightly aquiline, with the proud nostril open and well defined; dazzling teeth;—in short, her features had been faultless, but that her mouth is a little too large—but then, to amend that, her lips are like coral: and a more perfect figure I never beheld. Zah,gah,see,ga,qua is on a less scale, and her features more decidedly Indian.

We had a small, but compact and well-built boat, the seats of which we covered with mats, blankets, buffalo skins, cloaks, shawls, &c.: we had four voyageurs, Masta, Content, Le Blanc, and Pierrot; a very different set from those who brought me from Mackinaw: they were all Canadian voyageurs of the true breed, that is, half-breed, showing the Indian blood as strongly as the French. Pierrot, worthy his name, was a most comical fellow; Masta, a great talker, amused me exceedingly; Content was our steersman and captain; and Le Blanc, who was the best singer, generally led the song, to which the others responded in chorus.

They had a fixed daily allowance of fat pork, Indian meal, and tobacco: finding that the latter was not agreeable to me, though I took care not to complain, they always contrived, with genuine politeness, to smoke out of my way, and to leeward.

After passing Sugar Island, we took the channel to the left, and entered the narrow part of the lake between St. Joseph's Island and the main land. We dined upon a small picturesque islet, consisting of ledges of rock, covered with shrubs and abounding with whortle-berries; on the upper platform we arranged an awning or shade, by throwing a sail over some bushes, and made a luxuriant dinner, succeeded by a basin of good tea; meantime, on the rocky ledge below, Pierrot was making a *galette*, and Masta frying pork.

Dinner being over, we proceeded, coasting along the north shore of St. Joseph's Island. There is, in the interior, an English settlement, and a village of Indians. The principal proprietor, Major R——, who is a magistrate and justice of the peace, has two Indian women living with him—two sisters, and a family by each!—such are the examples sometimes set to the Indians on our frontiers.

In the evening we came to an island consisting of a flat ledge of rock, on which were the remains of a former camp-fire, surrounded by tall trees and bushes: here we pitched our little marquée, and boiled our kettle. The sun-set was most glorious, with some floating ominous clouds. The stars and the fire-flies came out together: the latter swarmed around us, darting in and out among the trees, and gliding and sparkling over the surface of the water. Unfortunately the mosquitoes swarmed too, notwithstanding the antipathy which is said to exist between the mosquito and the fire-fly. We made our beds by spreading mats and blankets under us; and then, closing the curtain of the tent, Mr. MacMurray began a very effective slaughter and expulsion of the mosquitoes. We laid ourselves down, Mrs. MacMurray in the middle, with her child in her bosom; Mr. MacMurray on one side, myself on the other, and the two Indian girls at our feet: the voyageurs, rolled in their blankets, lay upon the naked rock round the fire we had built—and thus we all slept. I must needs confess that I found my rocky bed rather uneasy, and my bones ached as I turned from side to side, but this was only a beginning. The night was close and sultry, and just before dawn I was wakened by a tremendous clap of thunder; down came the storm in its fury, the lake swelling and roaring, the lightning gambolling over the rocks and waves, the rain falling in a torrent; but we were well sheltered, for the men had had the precaution, before they slept, to throw a large oil cloth over the top of our little marquée. The storm ceased suddenly; daylight came, and soon afterwards we again embarked. We had made forty-five miles.

The next morning was beautiful: the sun shone brightly, though the lake was yet heaving and swelling from the recent storm,—altogether it was like the laughing eyes and pouting lips of a half-appeased beauty. About nine o'clock we ran down into a lovely bay, and landed to breakfast on a little lawn surrounded by high trees and a thick wood, abounding in rattlesnakes and squirrels. Luckily for us, the storm had dispersed the mosquitoes.

Keeping clear of the covert to avoid these fearful snakes, I strayed down by the edge of the lake, and found a tiny creek, which answered all purposes, both of bath and mirror, and there I arranged my toilette in peace and security. Returning to our breakfast-fire, I stood some moments to admire the group around it—it was a perfect picture: there lay the little boat rocking on the shining waves, and near it Content was washing plates and dishes; Pierrot and Masta were cooking; the two Indian girls were spreading the tablecloth on the turf. Mrs. MacMurray and her baby—looking like the Madonna and child in the "Repose in Egypt"—were seated under a tree; while Mr. MacMurray, having suspended his shaving-glass against the trunk of a pine, was shaving himself with infinite gravity and *sangfroid*. Never, I think, were the graceful, the wild, the comic, so strangely combined!—add the rich back-ground of mingled foliage, the murmur of leaves and waters, and all the glory of a summer morning!—it was very beautiful!

We breakfasted in much mirth, and then we set off again.

The channel widened, the sky became overcast, the wind freshened, and at length blew hard. Though this part of the lake is protected by St. Joseph's and the chain of islands from the swell of the main lake, still the waves rose high, the wind increased, we were obliged to take in a reef or two of our sail, and scudded with an almost fearful rapidity before the wind. In crossing a wide, open expanse of about twenty miles, we became all at once very silent, then very grave, then very pathetic, and at last extremely sick.

On arriving among the channels of the Rattlesnake Islands, the swell of course subsided; we landed on a most beautiful mass of rock, and lighted our fire under a group of pines and sycamores; but we were too sick to eat. Mr. MacMurray heated some port wine and water, into which we broke biscuit, and drank it most picturesquely out of a slop basin—too thankful to get it! Thus recruited, we proceeded. The wind continued fresh and fair, the day kept up fine, and our sail was most delightful and rapid. We passed successive groups of islands, countless in number, various in form, little fairy Edens—populous with life and love, and glowing with light and colour under a meridian sun. I remember we came into a circular basin, of about three miles in diameter, so surrounded with islands, that when once within the circle, I could perceive neither ingress nor egress; it was as if a spell of enchantment had been wrought to keep us there for ever; and I really thought we were going with our bows upon the rocks, when suddenly we darted through a narrow portal, not above two or three yards in width, and found ourselves in another wide expanse, studded with larger islands. At evening we entered the Missasagua river, having come sixty miles, right before the wind, since morning.

The Missasagua (*i.e.* the river with two mouths) gave its name to a tribe of the Chippewa nation, once numerous and powerful, now scattered and degraded. This is the river called by Henry the *Missasaki*, where he found a horde of Indians who had never seen a white man before, and who, in the excess of their hospitality, crammed him with "a porridge of sturgeon's roe," which I apprehend, from his description, would be likely to prove "*caviare* to the general." There is a remnant of these Indians here still. We found a log-hut with a half-breed family, in the service of the Fur Company; and two or three bark wigwams. The rest of the village, (dwellings and inhabitants together,) had gone down to the Manitoolin. A number of little Red-skins were running about, half, or rather indeed wholly, naked—happy, healthy, active, dirty little urchins, resembling, except in colour, those you may see swarming in an Irish cabin. Poor Ireland! The worst Indian wigwam is not worse than some of her dwellings; and the most miserable of these Indians would spurn the destiny of an Irish *poor-slave*—for he is at least lord o'er himself. As the river is still famous for sturgeon, we endeavoured to procure some for supper, and had just prepared a large piece to roast, (suspended by a cord to three sticks,) when one of those horrid curs so rife about the Indian dwellings ran off with it. We were asked to take up our night's lodging in the log-hut, but it was so abominably dirty and close, we all preferred the shore. While they pitched the marquée, I stood for some time looking at a little Indian boy, who, in a canoe about eight feet in length, was playing the most extraordinary gambols in the water; the buoyant thing seemed alive beneath him, and to obey every movement of his paddle. He shot backwards and forwards, described circles, whirled himself round and round, made pirouettes, exhibited, in short, as many tricks as I have seen played by a spirited English boy on a thorough-bred pony.

The mosquitoes were in great force, but we began by sweeping them out of the tent with boughs, and then closing the curtain, we executed judgment on the remainder by wholesale. We then lay down in the same order as last night; and Mrs. MacMurray sang her little boy to sleep with a beautiful hymn. I felt all the luxury of having the turf under me instead of the rock, and slept well till wakened before dawn by some animal sniffing and snuffing close to my ear. I commanded my alarm, and did not disturb those who were enjoying a sound sleep near me, and the intruder turned out to be a cow belonging to the hut, who had got her nose under the edge of the tent. We set off early, and by sunrise had passed down the eastern channel of the river, and swept into the lake. It was a lovely morning, soft and calm; there was no breath of wind; no cloud in the sky, no vapour in the air; and the little islands lay around "under the opening eyelids of the morn," dewy, and green, and silent. We made eighteen miles before breakfast; and then pursued our way through Aird's bay, and among countless islands of all shapes and sizes; I cannot describe their beauty, nor their harmonious variety; at last we perceived in the east the high ridge called the mountains of La Cloche. They are really respectable hills in this level country, but hardly mountains: they are all of lime-stone, and partially clothed in wood. All this coast is very rocky and barren; but it is said to be rich in mineral productions. About five in the evening we landed at La Cloche.

Here we found the first and only signs of civilized society during our voyage. The North-West Company have an important station here; and two of their principal clerks, Mr. MacBean and Mr. Bethune, were on the spot. We were received with much kindness, and pressed to spend the night, but there was yet so much daylight, and time was so valuable, that we declined. The factory consists of a large log-house, with extensive store to contain the goods bartered with the Indians, and huts inhabited by work people, hunters, voyageurs, and others; a small village, in short; and a number of boats and canoes of all sizes were lying in the bay. It is not merely the love of gain that induces well-educated men —gentlemen—to pass twenty years of their lives in such a place as this; you must add to the prospective acquirement of a large fortune, two possessions which men are most wont to covet—power and freedom. The table was laid in their hall for supper, and we carried off, with their good-will, a large mess of broiled fish, dish and all, and a can of milk, which delicious viands we discussed in our boat with great satisfaction.

The place derives its name from a large rock, which they say, being struck, vibrates like a bell. But I had no opportunity of trying the experiment, therefore cannot tell how this may be. Henry, however, mentions this phenomenon; and the Indians regard the spot as sacred and enchanted. Just after sunset, we reached one of the most enchanting of these enchanting or enchanted isles. It rose sloping from the shore, in successive ledges of picturesque rocks, all fringed with trees and bushes, and clothed in many places with a species of gray lichen, nearly a foot deep. With a sort of anticipative wisdom (like that of a pig in a storm) I gathered a quantity of this lichen for our bed, and spread it under the mats; for, in fear of the rattle-snakes and other creeping things, we had pitched our resting place on the naked rock. The men had built up the fire in a sheltered place below, and did not perceive that a stem of a blasted pine, about twenty feet in length, had fallen across the recess; it caught the flame. This at first delighted us and the men too, but soon it communicated to another tree against which it was leaning, and they blazed away together in a column of flame. We began to fear that it might communicate to the dried moss and the bushes, and cause a general conflagration; the men prevented this, however, by clearing a space around them. The waves, the trees and bushes and fantastic rocks, and the figures and faces of the men, caught the brilliant light as it flashed upon them with a fitful glare—the rest being lost in deepest shadow. Wildly magnificent it was! beyond all expression beautiful, and awful too!—the night, the solitude, the dark weltering waters, the blaze which put out the mild stars which just before had looked down upon us in their tender radiance!—I never beheld such a scene. By the light of this gigantic torch we supped and prepared our beds. As I lay down to rest, and closed my eyes on the flame which shone through our tent curtain, I thought that perhaps the wind might change in the night, and the flakes and sparks be carried over to us, and to the beds of lichen, dry and inflammable as tinder; but fatigue had subdued me so utterly, that even this apprehension could not keep me awake. I pressed my hands on my eyes, breathed my prayer, and slept in peace.

The burning trees were still smouldering; daylight was just creeping up the sky, and some few stars yet out, when we bestirred ourselves, and in a very few minutes we were again afloat; we were now steering towards the south-east, where the great Manitoolin Island was dimly discerned. There was a deep slumbrous calm all around, as if Nature had not yet awoke from her night's rest: then the atmosphere began to kindle with gradual light; it grew brighter and brighter: towards the east, the lake and sky were intermingling in radiance; and *then*, just there, where they seemed flowing and glowing together like a bath of fire, we saw what seemed to us the huge black hull of a vessel, with masts and spars rising against the sky—but we knew not what to think or to believe! As we kept on rowing in that direction, it grew more distinct, but lessened in size; it proved to be a great heavy-built schooner, painted black, which was going up the lake against wind and current. One man was standing in her bows, with an immense oar, which he slowly pulled, walking backwards and forwards; but vain seemed all his toil, for still the vessel lay like a black log, and moved not; we rowed up to the side, and hailed him—"What news?"

And the answer was that William the Fourth was dead, and that Queen Victoria reigned in his place! We sat silent looking at each other, and even in that very moment the orb of the sun rose out of the lake, and poured its beams full in our dazzled eyes.

We asked if the governor were at the Manitoolin Island? No; he was not there; but the chief officer of the Indian department had come to represent him, and the presents were to be given out to the assembled Indians this morning. We urged the men to take to their oars with spirit, and held our course due east down by the woody shores of this immense islands, among fields of reeds and rushes, and almost under the shadow of the towering forests.

Meantime, many thoughts came into my mind—some tears too into my eyes—not certainly for that dead king, who in ripe age and in all honour was gathered to the tomb—but for that living queen, so young and fair—

> "As many hopes hang on that noble head
> As there hang blosoms on the boughs in May!"

And what will become of *them*—of *her*! The idea that even here, in this new world of woods and waters, amid these remote wilds, to her so utterly unknown, her power reaches and her sovereignty is acknowledged, filled me with compassionate awe. I say *compassionate*, for if she feel in their whole extent the liabilities of her position, alas for her! And if she feel them not!—O worse and worse!

I tried to recall her childish figure and features. I thought over all I had heard concerning her. I thought she was not such a thing as they could make a mere pageant of; for *that* there is too much within—too little without. And what *will* they make of her? For at eighteen she will hardly make anything of them—I mean of the men and women round her. It is of the woman I think, more than of the queen; for as a part of the state machinery, she will do quite as well as another—better, perhaps: so far her youth and sex are absolutely in her favour, or rather in *our* favour. If she be but simple-minded, and true-hearted, and straightforward, with the common portion of intellect—if a royal education have not blunted in her the quick perceptions and pure kind instincts of the woman—if she has only had fair play, and carries into business plain distinct notions of right and wrong —and the fine moral sense that is not to be confounded by diplomatic verbiage and expediency—she will do better for us than a whole cabinet full of cut-and-dried officials, with Talleyrand at the head of them. And what a fair heritage is this which has fallen to her! A land young like herself—a land of hopes—and fair, most fair! Does she knew—does she care anything about it?—while hearts are beating warm for her, and voices bless her—and hands are stretched out towards her—even from these wild lake shores?

These thoughts were in my mind, or something like to these, as with aid of sail and oar we were gliding across the bay of Manitoolin. This bay is about three miles wide at the entrance, and runs about twelve miles in depth, in a southern direction. As we approached the farther end, we discerned the whole line of shore, rising in bold and beautiful relief from the water, to be covered with wigwams, and crowded with Indians. Suddenly we came to a little opening or channel, which was not visible till we were just upon it, and rounding a promontory, to my infinite delight and surprise, we came upon an unexpected scene,—a little bay within the bay. It was a beautiful basin, nearly an exact circle, of about three miles in circumference; in the centre lay a little wooded island, and all around, the shores rose sloping from the margin of the lake, like an amphitheatre, covered with wigwams and lodges, thick as they could stand amid intermingled trees; and beyond these arose the tall pine forest crowning and enclosing the whole. Some hundred canoes were darting hither and thither on the waters, or gliding along the shore, and a beautiful schooner lay against the green bank—its tall masts almost mingling with the forest trees, and its white sails half furled and half gracefully drooping.

We landed, and were received with much politeness by Mr. Jarvis, the chief superintendent of Indian affairs, and by Major Anderson, the Indian agent; and a space was cleared to pitch our tent, until room could be made for our accommodation in one of the government log-houses.

"Had I plantation of this isle, my lord,
And were the king of it, what would I do?
. . . . No kind of traffic
Would I admit;—no name of magistrate;
Letters should not be known; no use of service,
Of riches or of poverty—
. . . All men idle—all.
I would with such perfection govern, sir,
T' excel the golden age."

THE TEMPEST.

The word Manitoolin is a corruption or frenchification of the Indian *Manito,a,wahn,ing,* which signifies the "dwelling of spirits." They have given this name to a range of islands in Lake Huron, which extend from the channel of St. Mary's river nearly to Cape Hurd, a distance of about two hundred miles. Between this range of islands and the shore of the main land, there is an archipelago, consisting of many thousand islands or islets.*

The Great Manitoolin, on which I now am, is, according to the last survey, ninety-three miles in length, but very narrow, and so deeply and fantastically indented with gulfs and bays, that it was supposed to consist of many distinct islands. This is the second year that the presents to the Indians have been issued on this spot. The idea of forming on the Great Manitoolin a settlement of the Indians, and inviting those tribes scattered round the lakes to adopt it as a residence, has been for the last few years entertained by the Indian department; I say for the last few years, because it did not originate with the present governor; though I believe it has his entire approbation, as a means of removing them more effectually from all contact with the white settlers. It is objected to this measure that by cutting off the Indians from agricultural pursuits, and throwing them back upon their habits of hunting and fishing, it will retard their civilization; that removing them from the reserved land among the whites, their religious instruction will be rendered a matter

* The islands which fringe the north shores of Lake Huron from Lake George to Penetanguishine have been estimated by Lieut. Bayfield (in his official survey) at upwards of thirty-three thousand.

of difficulty; that the islands, being masses of barren rock, are almost incapable of cultivation; and that they are so far north-west, that it would be difficult to raise even a little Indian corn: * and hence the plan of settling the Indians here has been termed *unjustifiable*.

It is true that the smaller islands are rocky and barren; but the Great Manitoolin, Drummond's, and St. Joseph's, are fertile. The soil on which I now tread is rich and good; and all the experiments in cultivation already tried here have proved successful. As far as I can judge, the intentions of the government are benevolent and *justifiable*. There are a great number of Indians, Ottawas and Pottowattomies, who receive annual presents from the British government, and are residing on the frontiers of the American settlements, near Lake Michigan. These people, having disposed of their lands, know not where to go, and it is the wish of our government to assemble all those Indians who are our allies, and receive our annual presents, within the limits of the British territory—and this for reasons which certainly do appear very *reasonable* and politic.

There are three thousand seven hundred Indians, Ottawas, Chippewas, Pottowattomies, Winnebagoes, and Menomonies, encamped around us. The issue of the presents has just concluded, and appears to have given universal satisfaction; yet, were you to see their trifling nature, you would wonder that they think it worth while to travel from one to five hundred miles or more to receive them; and by an ordinance of the Indian department, every individual must present himself *in person* to receive the allotted portion. The common equipment of each chief or warrior (that is, each man) consists of three quarters of a yard of blue cloth, three yards of linen, one blanket, half an ounce of thread, four strong needles, one comb, one awl, one butcher's knife, three pounds of tobacco, three pounds of ball, nine pounds of shot, four pounds of powder, and six flints. The equipment of a woman consists of one yard and three quarters of coarse woollen, two yards and a half of printed calico, one blanket, one ounce of thread, four needles, one comb, one awl, one knife. For each child

* It appears, however, from the notes of the missionary Elliott, that a great number of Ottawas and Potoganatees had been residing on the Great Manitoolin two or three years previous to 1834, and had cultivated a portion of land.

there was a portion of woollen cloth and calico. Those chiefs who had been wounded in battle, or had extraordinary claims, had some little articles in extra quantity, and a gay shawl or handkerchief. To each principal chief of a tribe, the allotted portion of goods for his tribe was given, and he made the distribution to his people individually; and such a thing as injustice or partiality on one hand, or a murmur of dissatisfaction on the other, seemed equally unknown. There were, besides, extra presents of flags, medals, chiefs' guns, rifles, trinkets, brass kettles, the choice and distribution of which were left to the superintendent, with this proviso, that the expense on the whole was never to exceed nine pounds sterling for every one hundred chiefs or warriors.

While the Indians remain on the island, which is generally about five days, they receive rations of Indian corn and tallow, (fat melted down;) with this they make a sort of soup, boiling the Indian corn till it is of the consistence of porridge—then adding a handful of tallow and some salt, and stirring it well. Many a kettleful of this delectable mess did I see made, without feeling any temptation to taste it; but Major Anderson says it is not so *very* bad, when a man is *very* hungry, which I am content to believe on his testimony. On this and on the fish of the bay they live while here.

As soon as the distribution of the presents was over, a grand council of all the principal chiefs was convened, that they might be informed of the will of their great father.

You must understand, that on the promontory I have mentioned as shutting in the little bay on the north side, there are some government edifices; one large house, consisting of one room, as accommodation for the superintendent and officers; also a carpenter's house and a magazine for the stores and presents, all of logs. A deal plank raised on tressels served as a table; there were a few stools and benches of deal-board, and two raised wooden platforms for beds: such were the furniture and decorations of the grand council-hall in which the *representative* of the representative of their Great Mother had now assembled her red children; a flag was displayed in front upon a lofty pole—a new flag, with a new device, on which I saw troops of Indians gazing with much curiosity and interest, and the meaning of which was now to be explained to them.

The council met about noon. At the upper end of the log-house I have mentioned, stood the chief superintendent, with his secretary or grand vizier, Major Anderson; the two interpreters, and some other officials. At some little distance I sat with Mr. and Mrs. MacMurray, and a young son of the lieutenant governor; near me I perceived three Methodist missionaries and two Catholic priests. The chiefs came in, one after another, without any order of precedence. All those whom I had seen at Mackinaw recognized me immediately, and their dusky faces brightened as they held out their hands with the customary *bojou!* There was my old acquaintance the Rain, looking magnificent, and the venerable old Ottawa chief, Kish,ke,nick, (the Cut-hand.) The other remarkable chiefs of the Ottawas were Gitchee, Mokomaun, (the Great or Long-knife;) So,wan,quet, (the Forked-tree;) Kim,e,ne,-chau,zun, (the Bustard;) Mokomaun,ish, (the Bad-knife;) Pai,-mau,se,gai, (the Sun's course in a cloudless sky,) and As,si,-ke,nack, (the Black-bird;) the latter a very remarkable man, of whom I shall have to say more presently. Of the Chippewas, the most distinguished chiefs were, Aisence, (the Little Clam;) Wai,sow,win,de,bay, (the Yellow-head), and Shin,gua,conse, (the Pine;) these three are Christians. There were besides Ken,ne,bec,ano, (the Snake's-tail;) Muc,konce,e,wa,yun, (the Cub's-skin;) and two others whose style was quite grandiloquent,—Tai,bau,se,gai, (Bursts of Thunder at a distance,) and Me,twai,crush,kau, (the Sound of Waves breaking on the rocks.)

Nearly opposite to me was a famous Pottowattomi chief and conjurer, called the Two Ears. He was most fantastically dressed and hideously painted, and had two large clusters of swansdown depending from each ear—I suppose in illustration of his name. There were three men with their faces blacked with grease and soot, their hair dishevelled, and their whole appearance studiously squalid and miserable: I was told they were in mourning for near relations. With these exceptions the dresses were much what I have already described; but the chief whom I immediately distinguished from the rest, even before I knew his name, was my cousin, young Waub-Ojeeg, the son of Wayish,ky; in height he towered above them all, being about six feet three or four.

His dress was equally splendid and tasteful; he wore a surtout of fine blue cloth, under which was seen a shirt of gay colours, and his father's medal hung on his breast. He had a magnificent embroidered belt of wampum, from which hung his scalping-knife and pouch. His leggings (metasses) were of scarlet cloth, beautifully embroidered, with rich bands or garters depending to his ankle. Round his head was an embroidered band or handkerchief, in which were stuck four wing-feathers of the war-eagle, two on each side—testimonies of his prowess as a warrior. He held a tomahawk in his hand. His features were fine, and his countenance not only mild, but almost femininely soft. Altogether he was in dress and personal appearance the finest specimen of his race I had yet seen; I was quite proud of my adopted kinsman.

He was seated at some distance; but in far too near propinquity, for in truth they almost touched me, sat a group of creatures—human beings I must suppose them, such as had never been seen before within the lines of civilization. I had remarked them in the morning surrounded by a group of Ottawas, among whom they seemed to excite as much wonder and curiosity as among ourselves; and when I inquired who and what they were, I was told they were *cannibals* from the Red River, the title being, I suspect, quite gratuitous, and merely expressive of the disgust they excited. One man had his hair cut short on the top of his head, and it looked like a circular blacking-brush, while it grew long in a fringe all round, hanging on his shoulders. The skins thrown round them seemed on the point of rotting off; and their attitude, when squatted on the ground, was precisely that of the larger ape I have seen in a menagerie. More hideous, more pitiable specimens of humanity in its lowest, most degraded state, can hardly be conceived; melancholy, squalid, stupid—and yet not fierce. They had each received a kettle and a gun by way of encouragement.

The whole number of chiefs assembled was seventy-five; and take notice, that the half of them were smoking, that it was blazing noon-tide, and that every door and window was filled up with the eager faces of the crowd without, and then you may imagine that even a scene like this was not to be enjoyed without some drawbacks; in fact, it was a sort of purgatory to more senses than one, but I made up my mind to endure, and did so. I observed that although there were many hundreds round the house, not one woman, outside or inside, was visible during the whole time the council lasted.

When all were assembled, and had seated themselves on the floor, without hurry, noise, or confusion, there was a pause of solemn preparation, and then Mr. Jarvis rose and addressed them. At the end of every sentence, As,si,ke,nack, (the Black-bird,) our chief interpreter here, translated the meaning to the assembly, raising his voice to a high pitch, and speaking with much oratorical emphasis—the others responding at intervals, "Ha!" but listening generally in solemn silence. This man, the Black-bird, who understands English well, is the most celebrated orator of his nation. They relate with pride that on one occasion he began a speech at sunrise, and that it lasted, without intermission, till sunset: the longest breathed of our parliament orators must yield, I think, to the Black-bird.

The address of the superintendent was in these words:—

"*Children!*—When your Great Father, the lieutenant-governor, parted with his Red children last year at his place, he promised again to meet them here at the council-fire, and witness in person the grand delivery of presents now just finished.

"To fulfil this engagement, your Great Father left his residence at Toronto, and proceeded on his way to the Great Manitoolin Island, as far as Lake Simcoe. At this place, a messenger who had been despatched from Toronto overtook him, and informed him of the death of our Great Father, on the other side of the Great Salt Lake, and the accession of the Queen Victoria. It consequently became necessary for your Great Father, the lieutenant-governor, to return to the seat of his government, and hold a council with his chief men.

"*Children!*—Your Great Father, the lieutenant-governor, has deputed me to express to you his regret and disappointment at being thus unexpectedly deprived of the pleasure which he had promised to himself, in again seeing all his Red children, and in taking by the hand the chiefs and warriors of the numerous tribes now here assembled.

"*Children!*—I am now to communicate to you a matter in which many of you are deeply interested. Listen with attention, and bear well in mind what I say to you.

"*Children!*—Your Great Father the King had determined that presents should be continued to be given to all Indians resident in the Canadas.

"But presents will be given to Indians residing in the United States only for three years, including the present delivery.

"*Children!*—The reasons why presents will not be continued to the Indians residing in the United States I will explain to you.

"First: All our countrymen who resided in the United States forfeited their claim to protection from the British government, from the moment their Great Father the King lost possession of that country. Consequently the Indians have no right to expect that their Great Father will continue to them what he does not continue to his own white children.

"Secondly: The Indians of the United States who served in the late war have already received from the British government more than has been received by the soldiers of their Great Father, who have fought for him for twenty years.

"Thirdly: Among the rules which civilized nations are bound to attend to, there is one which forbids your Great Father to give arms and ammunition to Indians of the United States, who are fighting against the government under which they live.

"Fourthly: The people of England have, through their representatives in the great council of the nation, uttered great complaints at the expense attendant upon a continuation of the expenditure of so large a sum of money upon Indian presents.

"But, *Children!* let it be distinctly understood, that the British government has not come to a determination to cease to give presents to the Indians of the United States. On the contrary, the government of your Great Father will be most happy to do so, provided they live in the British empire. Therefore, although your Great Father is willing that his Red children should all become permanent settlers in the island, it matters not in what part of the British empire they reside. They may go across the Great Salt Lake to the country of their Great Father the King, and there reside, and there receive their presents; or they may remove to any part of the provinces of Upper or Lower Canada, New Brunswick, Nova Scotia, or any other British colony, and yet receive them.

But they cannot and must not expect to receive them after the end of three years, if they continue to reside within the limits of the United States.

"*Children!*—The Long Knives have complained (and with justice too) that your Great Father, whilst he is at peace with them, has supplied his Red children residing in their country, with whom the Long Knives are at war, with guns and powder and ball.

"*Children!*—This, I repeat to you, is against the rules of civilized nations, and if continued, will bring on war between your Great Father and the Long Knives.

"*Children!*—You must therefore come and live under the protection of your Great Father, or lose the advantage which you have so long enjoyed, of annually receiving valuable presents from him.

"*Children!*—I have one thing more to observe to you. There are many clergymen constantly visiting you for the avowed purpose of instructing you in religious principles. Listen to them with attention when they talk to you on that subject; but at the same time keep always in view, and bear it well in your minds, that they have nothing whatever to do with your temporal affairs. Your Great Father who lives across the Great Salt Lake is your guardian and protector, and he only. He has relinquished his claim to this large and beautiful Island, on which we are assembled, in order that you may have a home of your own quite separate from his white children. The soil is good, and the waters which surround the shores of this island are abundantly supplied with the finest fish. If you cultivate the soil with only moderate industry, and exert yourselves to obtain fish, you can never want, and your Great Father will continue to bestow annually on all those who permanently reside here, or in any part of his dominions, valuable presents, and will from time to time visit you at this island, to behold your improvements.

"*Children!*—Your Great Father, the lieutenant-governor, as a token of the above declaration, transmits to the Indians a silk British flag, which represents the British empire. Within this flag, and immediately under the symbol of the British crown, are delineated a British lion and a beaver; by which is designated that the British people and the Indians, the former being represented by the lion and the latter by the beaver, are, and will be, alike regarded by their sovereign, so long as their figures are imprinted on the British flag, or, in other words, so long as they continue to inhabit the British empire.

"*Children!*—This flag is now yours. But it is necessary that some one tribe should take charge of it, in order that it may be exhibited in this island on all occasions, when your Great Father either visits or bestows presents on his Red children. Choose, therefore, from among you, the tribe to which you are willing to entrust it for safe-keeping, and remember to have it with you when we next meet again at this place.

"*Children!*—I bid you farewell. But before we part, let me express to you the high satisfaction I feel at witnessing the quiet, sober, and orderly conduct which has prevailed in the camp since my arrival. There are assembled here upwards of three thousand persons, composed of different tribes. I have not seen nor heard of any wrangling or quarrelling among you; I have not seen even one man, woman, or child, in a state of intoxication.

"*Children!*—Let me entreat you to abstain from indulging in the use of fire-water. Let me entreat you to return immediately to your respective homes, with the presents now in your possession. Let me warn you against attempts that may be made by traders or other persons to induce you to part with your presents, in exchange for articles of little value. —Farewell."

When Mr. Jarvis ceased speaking, there was a pause, and then a fine Ottawa chief (I think Mokomaun,ish) arose, and spoke at some length. He said, that with regard to the condition on which the presents would be issued in future, they would deliberate on the affair, and bring their answer next year.

Shinguaconse then came forward and made a long and emphatic speech, from which I gathered that he and his tribe requested that the principal council-fire might be transferred to St. Mary's River, and objected to a residence on the Manitoolin Island. After him spoke two other chiefs, who signified their entire acquiescence in what their Great Father had advised, and declared themselves satisfied to reside on the Manitoolin Islands.

After some deliberation among themselves, the custody of the flag was consigned to the Ottawa tribe then residing on the island, and to their principal chief, who came forward and received it with great ceremony.

There was then a distribution of extra presents, medals, silver gorgets, and amulets, to some of the chiefs and relatives of chiefs whose conduct was particularly approved, or whom it was thought expedient to gratify.

The council then broke up, and I made my way into the open air as quickly as I could.

On the 6th of August I bade adieu to my good friends Mr. and Mrs. MacMurray. I had owed too much to their kindness to part from them without regret. They returned up the lake, with their beautiful child and Indian retinue, to St. Mary's, while I prepared to embark in a canoe with the superintendent, to go down the lake to Penetanguishine, a voyage of four days at least, supposing wind and weather to continue favourable. Thence to Toronto, across Lake Simcoe, was a journey of three days more. Did I not say Providence took care of me? Always I have found efficient protection when I most needed and least expected it; and nothing could exceed the politeness of Mr. Jarvis and his people;—it *began* with politeness,—but it ended with something more and better—real and zealous kindness.

Now, to take things in order, and that you may accompany us in our canoe voyage, I must describe in the first place our arrangements. You shall confess ere long that the Roman emperor who proclaimed a reward for the discovery of a new pleasure, ought to have made a voyage down Lake Huron in a birch-bark canoe.

There were two canoes, each five-and-twenty feet in length, and four feet in width, tapering to the two extremities, and light, elegant, and buoyant as the sea-mew when it skims the summer waves: in the first canoe were Mr. Jarvis and myself, the governor's son, a lively boy of fourteen or fifteen, old Solomon the interpreter, and seven voyageurs. My blankets and night-gear being rolled up in a bundle, served for a seat, and I had a pillow at my back; and thus I reclined in the bottom of the canoe, as in a litter, very much at my ease: my companions were almost equally comfortable. I had near me my cloak, umbrella, and parasol, my note-books and sketch-books, and a little compact basket always by my side, containing eau de Cologne, and all those necessary luxuries which might be wanted in a moment, for I was well resolved that I would occasion no trouble but what was inevitable. The voyageurs were disposed on low wooden seats, suspended to the ribs of the canoe, except our Indian steersman, Martin, who, in a cotton shirt, arms bared to the shoulder, loose trowsers, a scarlet sash round his waist, richly embroidered with beads, and his long black hair waving, took his place in the stern, with a paddle twice as long as the others.*

The manner in which he stood, turning and twisting himself with the lithe agility of a snake, and striking first on one side, then on the other, was very graceful and picturesque. So much depends on the skill, and dexterity, and intelligence of these steersmen, that they have always double pay. The other men were all picked men, Canadian half-breeds, young, well-looking, full of glee and good-nature, with untiring arms and more untiring lungs and spirits; a handkerchief twisted round the head, a shirt and pair of trowsers, with a gay sash, formed the prevalent costume. We had on board a canteen, and other light baggage, two or three guns, and fishing tackle.

The other canoe carried part of Mr. Jarvis's retinue, the heavy baggage, provisions, marquees, guns, &c., and was equipped with eight paddles. The party consisted altogether of twenty-two persons, viz: twenty-one men, and myself, the only woman.

We started off in swift and gallant style, looking grand and official, with the British flag floating at our stern. Major Anderson and his people, and the schooner's crew, gave us three cheers. The Indians uttered their wild cries, and discharged their rifles all along the shore. As we left the bay, I counted seventy-two canoes before us, already on their homeward voyage—some to the upper waters of the lake—some to the northern shores; as we passed them, they saluted us by discharging their rifles: the day was without a cloud, and it was altogether a most animated and beautiful scene.

I forgot to tell you that the Indians are very fond of having pet animals in their wigwams,—not only dogs, but tame foxes and hawks. Mr. Jarvis purchased a pair of young

* The common paddle (called by the Canadians *aviron*, and by the Indians *admee*) is about two feet and a half long.

hawks, male and female, from an Indian, intending them for his children. Just as we left the island, one of these birds escaped from the basket, and flew directly to the shore of the bay, where it was lost in the thick forest. We proceeded, and after leaving the bay about twelve miles onwards, we landed on a little rocky island: some one heard the cry of a hawk over our heads; it was the poor bird we had lost; he had kept his companion in sight all the way, following us unseen along the shore, and now suffered himself to be taken and caged with the other.

We bought some black-bass from an Indian who was spearing fish: and, *a-propos!* I never yet have mentioned what is one of the greatest pleasures in the navigation of these magnificent upper lakes—the purity, the coldness, the transparency of the water. I have been told that if in the deeper parts of the lake a white handkerchief be sunk with the lead, it is distinctly visible at a depth of thirty fathoms—we did not try the experiment, not being in deep water; but here, among shoals and islands, I could almost always see the rocky bottom, with glittering pebbles, and the fish gliding beneath us with their waving fins and staring eyes—and if I took a glass of water, it came up sparkling as from the well at Harrowgate, and the flavour was delicious. You can hardly imagine how much this added to the charm and animation of the voyage.

About sunset, we came to the hut of a fur trader, whose name, I think, was Lemorondière: it was on the shore of a beautiful channel running between the main land and a large island. On a neighbouring point, Wai,sow,win,de,bay (the Yellow-head) and his people were building their wigwams for the night. The appearance was most picturesque, particularly when the camp fires were lighted and the night came on. I cannot forget the figure of a squaw, as she stood, dark and tall, against the red flames, bending over a great black kettle, her blanket trailing behind her, her hair streaming on the night breeze;—most like to one of the witches in Macbeth.

We supped here on excellent trout and white-fish, but sand-flies and mosquitoes were horridly tormenting; the former, which are so diminutive as to be scarcely visible, were by far the worst. We were off next morning by daylight, the Yellow-head's people discharging their rifles by way of salute.

The voyageurs measure the distance by *pipes*. At the end of a certain time there is a pause, and they light their pipes and smoke for about five minutes, then the paddles go off merrily again, at the rate of about fifty strokes in a minute, and we absolutely seem to fly over the water. "*Trois* pipes," are about twelve miles. We breakfasted this morning on a little island of exceeding beauty, rising precipitately from the water. In front we had the open lake, lying blue, and bright, and serene, under the morning sky, and the eastern extremity of the Manitoolin Island; and islands all around as far as we could see. The feeling of remoteness, of the profound solitude, added to the sentiment of beauty: it was Nature in her first freshness and innocence, as she came from the hand of her Maker, and before she had been sighed upon by humanity—defiled at once, and sanctified by the contact. Our little island abounded with beautiful shrubs, flowers, green mosses, and scarlet lichens. I found a tiny recess, where I made my bath and toilette very comfortably. On returning, I found breakfast laid on a piece of rock; my seat, with my pillow and cloak all nicely arranged, and a bouquet of flowers lying on it. This was a never-failing *gallanterie*, sometimes from one, sometimes from another, of my numerous *cavaliers*.

This day we had a most delightful run among hundreds of islands; sometimes darting through narrow rocky channels, so narrow that I could not see the water on either side of the canoe; and then emerging, we glided through vast fields of white water-lilies; it was perpetual variety, perpetual beauty, perpetual delight and enchantment, from hour to hour. The men sang their gay French songs, the other canoe joining in the chorus.

This peculiar singing has often been described; it is very animated on the water and in the open air, but not very harmonious. They all sing in unison, raising their voices and marking the time with their paddles. One always led, but in these there was a diversity of taste and skill. If I wished to hear "*En roulant ma boule, roulette,*" I applied to Le Duc. Jacques excelled in "*La belle rose blanche,*" and Louis was great in "*Trois canards s'en vont baignant.*"

They often amused me by a specimen of dexterity, something like that of an accomplished whip in London. They would paddle up towards the shore with such extreme velocity, that I expected to be dashed on the rock, and then in a moment, by a simultaneous back-stroke of the paddle, stop with a jerk, which made me breathless.

My only discomposure arose from the destructive propensities of the gentlemen, all keen and eager sportsmen; the utmost I could gain from their mercy was, that the fish should gasp to death out of my sight, and the pigeons and the wild ducks be put out of pain instantly. I will, however, acknowledge, that when the bass-fish and pigeons were produced, broiled and fried, they looked so *appétissants*, smelt so savoury, and I was *so* hungry, that I soon forgot all my sentimental pity for the victims.

We found to-day, on a rock, the remains of an Indian lodge, over which we threw a sail-cloth, and dined luxuriously on our fish and pigeons, and a glass of good madeira. After dinner, the men dashed off with great animation, singing my favourite ditty,

> Si mon moine voulait danser,
> Un beau cheval lui donnerai!

—through groups of lovely islands, sometimes scattered wide, and sometimes clustered so close, that I often mistook twenty or thirty together for one large island; but on approaching nearer, they opened before us, and appeared intersected by winding labyrinthine channels, where, amid flags and water-lilies, beneath the shade of rich embowering foliage, we glided on our way; and then we came upon a wide open space, where we could feel the heave of the waters under us, and across which the men—still singing with untiring vivacity—paddled with all their might to reach the opposite islands before sunset. The moment it becomes too dark for our steersman to see *through* the surface of the water, it becomes in the highest degree dangerous to proceed; such is the frail texture of these canoes, that a pin's point might scratch a hole in the bottom; a sunk rock, or a *snag* or projecting bough—and often we glided within an inch of them—had certainly swamped us.

We passed this day two Indian sepulchres, on a point of rock, overshadowed by birch and pine, with the sparkling waters murmuring round them; I landed to examine them. The Indians cannot here *bury* their dead, for there is not a sufficiency of earth to cover them from sight, but they lay the body, wrapped up carefully in bark, on the flat rock, and then cover it over with rocks and stones. This was the tomb of a woman and her child, and fragments of the ornaments and other things buried with them were still perceptible.

We landed at sunset on a flat ledge of rock, free from bushes, which we avoided as much as possible, from fear of mosquitoes and rattle-snakes; and while the men pitched the marquees and cooked supper, I walked and mused.

I wish I could give you the least idea of the beauty of this evening; but while I try to put in words what was before me, the sense of its ineffable loveliness overpowers me *now*, even as it did then. The sun had set in that cloudless splendour, and that peculiar blending of rose and amber light that belongs only to these climes and Italy; the lake lay weltering under the western sky like a bath of molten gold; the rocky islands which studded its surface were of a dense purple, except where their edges seemed fringed with fire. They assumed, to the visionary eye, strange forms; some were like great horned beetles, and some like turtles, and some like crocodiles, and some like sleeping whales, and winged fishes: the foliage upon them resembled dorsal fins, and sometimes tufts of feathers. Then, as the purple shadows came darkening from the east, the young crescent moon showed herself, flinging a paly splendour over the water. I remember standing on the shore, "my spirits as in a dream were all bound up"—overcome by such an intense feeling of *the beautiful*—such a deep adoration for the power that had created it,—I must have suffocated if——

But why tell *you* this?

They pitched my tent at a *respectful* distance from the rest, and Mr. Jarvis made me a delicious elastic bed of some boughs, over which was spread a bearskin, and over that blankets: but the night was hot and feverish. The voyageurs, after rowing since daylight, were dancing and singing on the shore till near midnight.

Next morning we were off again at early dawn, paddled "*trois* pipes" before breakfast, over an open space which they call a "traverse," caught eleven bass fish, and shot two pigeons. The island on which we breakfasted was in great part white marble; and in the clefts and hollows grew quantities of gooseberries and raspberries, wild-roses, the crimson columbine, a large species of harebell, a sort of willow, juniper birch, and stunted pine, and such was the usual vegetation.

It is beautiful to see in these islands the whole process of preparatory vegetation unfolded and exemplified before one's eyes—each successive growth preparing a soil for that which is to follow.

There was first the naked rock washed by the spray, where the white gulls were sitting: then you saw the rock covered with some moss or lichens; then, in the clefts and seams, some long grass, a few wild flowers and strawberries; then a few juniper and rose bushes; then the dwarf pine, hardly rising two or three feet; and lastly, trees and shrubs of large growth: and the nearer to the main land, the richer of course the vegetation, for the seeds are wafted thence by the winds, or carried by the birds, and so dispersed from island to island.

We landed to-day on the "Island of Skulls," an ancient sepulchre of the Hurons: some skulls and bones were scattered about, with the rough stones which had once been heaped over them. The spot was most wild and desolate, rising from the water edge in successive ledges of rock to a considerable height, with a few blasted gray pines here and there, round which several pairs of hawks were wheeling and uttering their shrill cry. We all declared we would not dine on this ominous island, and proceeded. We doubled a remarkable cape mentioned by Henry as the *Pointe aux Grondines*. There is always a heavy swell here, and a perpetual sound of breakers on the rocks, whence its name. Only a few years ago, a trader in his canoe, with sixteen people, were wrecked and lost on this spot.

We also passed within some miles of the mouth of the *Rivière des Français*, the most important of all the rivers which flow into Lake Huron. It forms the line of communication for the north-west traders from Montreal; the common route is up the Ottawa River, across Lake Nippissing, and down the River Français into Lake Huron, and by the Saulte Ste. Marie into Lake Superior. Pray have a map before you during this voyage.*

* This part of Lake Huron, and indeed all its upper shores, are very incorrectly laid down in Wyld's map of Upper Canada. Bouchette's large map, and also a beautiful small one published by Blackwood in 1833, are much more accurate.

Leaving behind this cape and river, we came again upon lovely groups of Elysian islands, channels winding among rocks and foliage, and more fields of water-lilies. In passing through a beautiful channel, I had an opportunity of seeing the manner in which an Indian communicates with his friends when *en route*. A branch was so arranged as to project far across the water and catch the eye: in a cleft at the extremity a piece of birch-bark was stuck with some hieroglyphic marks scratched with red ochre, of which we could make nothing—one figure, I thought, represented a fish.

To-day we caught several bass, shot four pigeons, also a large water-snake—which last I thought a gratuitous piece of cruelty. We dined upon a large and picturesque island—large in comparison with those we usually selected, being perhaps two or three miles round; it was very woody and wild, intersected by deep ravines, and rising in bold, abrupt precipices. We dined luxriously under a group of trees: the heat was overpowering, and the mosquitoes very troublesome.

After dinner we pursued our course through an archipelago of islets, rising out of the blue waves, and fringed with white water-lilies;—little fairy Edens, of such endless variety in form and colour, and of such wondrous and fantastic beauty, I know not how to describe them.

We landed on one, where there was a rock so exactly resembling the head and part of a turtle, that I could have taken it for a sculpture. The Indians looked upon is as sacred, and it is customary for all who pass to leave an offering in money, tobacco, corn, &c., to the spirit. I duly left mine, but I could see by the laughing eyes of Jacques and Louis, that "the spirit" was not likely to be the better for my devotion.

Mr. Jarvis asked me to sing a French song for the voyageurs, and Louis looked back with his bright arch face, as much as to say, "Pray do," when a shout was heard from the other canoe, "A mink! A mink!"* and all the paddles were now in animated motion. We dashed up among the reeds, we chased the creature up and down, and at last to a hole under a rock; the voyageurs beat the reeds with their paddles, the gentlemen seized their guns; there were twenty-one men half frantic in pursuit of a wretched little creature, whose death could serve no purpose. It dived, but

* A species of otter.

rose a few yards farther, and was seen making for the land; a shot was fired, it sprang from the water; another, and it floated dead;—thus we repaid the beauty, and enjoyment, and lavish loveliness spread around us, with pain and with destruction.

I recollect that as we passed a lovely bit of an island, all bordered with flags and white lilies, we saw a beautiful wild duck emerge from a green covert, and lead into the lake a numerous brood of ducklings. It was a sight to touch the heart with a tender pleasure, and I pleaded hard, very hard, for mercy; but what thorough sportsman ever listened to such a word? The deadly guns were already levelled, and even while I spoke, the poor mother-bird was shot, and the little ones, which could not fly, went fluttering and scudding away into the open lake to perish miserably.

But what was really very touching was to see the poor gulls; sometimes we would startle a whole bevy of them as they were floating gracefully on the waves, and they would rise soaring away beyond our reach; but the voyageurs, suspending their paddles, imitated exactly their own soft low whistle; and then the wretched, foolish birds, just as if they had been so many women, actually wheeled round in the air, and came flying back to meet the "fiery death."

The voyageurs eat these gulls, in spite of their fishy taste, with great satisfaction.

I wonder how it is that some of those gentry whom I used to see in London, looking as though they would give an empire for a new pleasure or a new sensation, do not come here? If epicures, they should come to eat white-fish and beavers' tails; if sportsmen, here is a very paradise for bear-hunting, deer-hunting, otter-hunting; and wild-fowl in thousands, and fish in shoals; and if they be contemplative lovers of the picturesque, *blasés* with Italy and elbowed out of Switzerland, let them come here and find the true philosopher's stone—or rather the true elixir of life—*novelty!*

At sunset we encamped on a rocky island of most fantastic form, like a Z. They pitched my tent on a height, and close to the door was a precipitous descent into a hollow, where they lighted vast fires, and thus kept off the mosquitoes, which were in great force. I slept well, but towards morning some creature crept into my tent and over my bed —a snake, as I supposed; after this I slept no more.

We started at half-past four. Hitherto the weather had been glorious; but this morning the sun rose among red and black clouds, fearfully ominous. As we were turning a point under some lofty rocks, we heard the crack of a rifle, and saw an Indian leaping along the rocks, and down towards the shore. We rowed in, not knowing what it meant, and came upon a night-camp of Indians, part of the tribe of Aisence, (the Clam.) They had only hailed us to make some trifling inquiries; and I heard Louis, *sotto voce*, send them *au diable!* —for now the weather lowered darker and darker, and every moment was precious.

We breakfasted on an island almost covered with flowers, some gorgeous, and strange, and unknown, and others sweet and familiar; plenty of the wild-pea, for instance, and wild-roses, of which I had many offerings. I made my toilette in a recess among some rocks; but just as I was emerging from my primitive dressing-room, I felt a few drops of rain, and saw too clearly that our good fortune was at an end. We swallowed a hasty breakfast, and had just time to arrange ourselves in the canoe with all the available defences of cloaks and umbrellas, when the rain came down heavily and hopelessly. But notwithstanding the rain and the dark gray sky, the scenery was even more beautiful than ever. The islands were larger, and assumed a richer appearance; the trees were of more luxuriant growth, no longer the dwarfed pine, but lofty oak and maple. These are called the Bear Islands, from the number of those animals found upon them; old Solomon told me that an Indian whom he knew had shot nine bears in the course of a single day. We found three bears' heads stuck upon the boughts of a dead pine—probably as offerings to the souls of the slaughtered animals, or to the "Great Spirit," both being usual.

We dined on a wet rock, almost covered with that species of lichen which the Indians call wa,ac, and the Canadians *tripe de roche*, because, when boiled till soft, and then fried in grease, it makes a dish not unpalatable—when one has nothing else.* The Clam and some of his people landed and dined at the same time. After dinner the rain came on worse and worse. Old Solomon asked me once or twice how I felt;

* It is often mentioned in the Travels of Back and Franklin.

and I thought his anxiety for my health was caused by the rain; but no:—he told me that on the island where we had dined he had observed a great quantity of a certain plant, which, if only touched, causes a dreadful eruption and ulcer all over the body. I asked why he had not shown it to me, and warned me against it? and he assured me that such warning would only have increased the danger, for when there is any knowledge or apprehension of it existing in the mind, the very air blowing from it sometimes infects the frame. Here I appealed to Mr. Jarvis, who replied, "All I know is, that I once unconsciously touched a leaf of it, and became one ulcer from head to foot; I could not stir for a fortnight." *

This was a dreadful night, for the rain came on more violently, accompanied by a storm of wind. It was necessary to land and make our fires for the night. The good-natured men were full of anxiety and compassion for me, poor, lonely, shivering woman that I was in the midst of them! The first thought with every one was to place me under shelter, and my tent was pitched instantly with much zeal, and such activity, that the sense of inconvenience and suffering was forgotten in the thankful sense of kindness, and all things became endurable.

The tent was pitched on a height, so that the water ran off on all sides; I contrived for myself a dry bed, and Mr. Jarvis brought me some hot madeira. I rolled myself up in my German blanket, and fell into a deep, sound sleep. The voyageurs, who apparently need nothing but their own good spirits to feed and clothe them, lighted a great fire, turned the canoes upside down, and, sheltered under them, were heard singing and laughing during great part of this tempestuous night.

Next morning we were off by five o'clock. My beautiful lake looked horribly sulky, and all the little islands were lost in a cold gray vapour: we were now in the Georgian Bay. Through the misty atmosphere loomed a distant shore of

* I do not know the botanical name of this plant, which resembles a dwarf sumach: it was subsequently pointed out to me in the woods by a Methodist preacher, who told me that his daughter, merely by standing to windward of the plant while looking at it, suffered dreadfully. It is said that formerly the Indians used it to poison their arrows.

considerable height. Dupré told me that what I saw was the Isle des Chrétiens, and that formerly there was a large settlement of the Jesuits there, and that still there were to be seen the remains of "*une grande cathédrale*." About nine o'clock we entered the bay of Penetanguishine, so called from a high sand-bank at the entrance, which is continually crumbling away. The expressive Indian name signifies "Look! it is falling sand!"

We spent the greater part of two days at Penetanguishine, which is truly a most lovely spot. The bay runs up into the land like some of the Scottish lochs, and the shores are bolder and higher than usual, and as yet all clothed with the primeval forest. During the war there were dockyards and a military and naval depot here, maintained at an immense expense to government; and it is likely, from its position, to rise into a station of great importance; at present, the only remains of all the warlike demonstrations of former times are a sloop sunk and rotting in the bay, and a large stone building at the entrance, called the "Fort," but merely serving as barracks for a few soldiers from the garrison at Toronto. There are several pretty houses on the beautiful declivity, rising on the north side of the bay, and the families settled here have contrived to assemble round them many of the comforts and elegancies of life. I have reason to remember with pleasure a Russian lady, the wife of an English officer, who made my short sojourn here very agreeable.

There was an inn here, not the worst of Canadian inns; and the *wee* closet called a bed-room, and the little bed with its white cotton curtains, appeared to me the *ne plus ultra* of luxury. I recollect walking in and out of the room ten times a day for the mere pleasure of contemplating it, and anticipated with impatience the moment when I should throw myself down into it, and sleep once more on a Christian bed. But nine nights passed in the open air, or on rocks, and on boards, had spoiled me for the comforts of civilization, and to sleep *on a bed* was impossible: I was smothered, I was suffocated, and altogether wretched and fevered;—I sighed for my rock on Lake Huron.

At Penetanguishine there is a hamlet, consisting of

twenty or thirty log-houses, where a small remnant of the poor commuted pensioners (in all a hundred and twenty-six persons) now reside, receiving daily rations of food, and some little clothing, just sufficient to sustain life.

From some particular circumstances the case of these commuted pensioners was frequently brought under my observation while I was in Canada, and excited my strongest interest and compassion. I shall give you a brief sketch of this tragedy, for such it truly is; not by way of exciting sympathy, which can now avail nothing, but because it is in many points of view fraught with instruction.

The commuted pensioners were veteran soldiers, entitled to a small yearly pension for wounds or length of service, and who accepted the offer made to them by our government in 1832, to commute their pensions for four years' purchase, and a grant of one hundred acres of land in Canada.

The *intention* of the government seems to have been to send out able-bodied men, who would thus cease, after a few years, to be a burthen on the country. A part of the money due to them was to be deducted for their voyage and expenses out; of the remaining sum a part was to be paid in London, part at Quebec, and the rest when settled on the land awarded to them. These *intentions* sound well; unluckily they were not properly acted upon. Some received the whole of the money due to them in England, and drank themselves to death, or squandered it, and then refused to leave the country. Some drank themselves to death, or died of the cholera, at Quebec; and of those who came out, one half were described to me* as presenting a list of all the miseries and diseases incident to humanity—some with one arm, some with one leg, bent with old age or rheumatism, lame, halt, and even, will it be believed, blind!† And such were the men to be set down in the midst of the swamp and forest, there to live as they could. When some few, who had been more provident, presented themselves to the commissary at Toronto for payment of the rest of the money due to them, it was found that the proper papers had not been

* I have these particulars from the chief of the commissariat in Upper Canada, and the emigrant agent.

† One of these men, stone-blind, was begging in the streets of Toronto.

forwarded; they we written for to the Chelsea Board, which had to apply to the War-office, which had to apply to the Treasury: the papers, after being bandied about from office to office, from clerk to secretary, from secretary to clerk, were sent, at length, after a lapse of eight or ten months, during which time the poor men, worn out with suspense, had taken to begging, or to drinking, in utter despondency; and when the order for their money *did* at last arrive, they had become useless, abandoned creatures.

Those who were located were sent far up into the bush (there being no disposable government lands nearer,) where there were no roads, no markets for their produce if they *did* raise it; and in this new position, if their hearts did not sink, and their limbs fail at once, their ignorance of farming, their improvidence and helplessness, arising from the want of self-dependence, and the mechanical docility of military service, were moral obstacles stronger than any physical ones. The forest-trees they had to contend with were not more deeply rooted than the adverse habits and prejudices and infirmities they had brought with them.

According to the commissary, the number of those who commuted their pensions was about twelve hundred. Of these it is calculated that eight hundred reached Upper Canada: of these eight hundred, not more than four hundred and fifty are now living; and of these, some are begging through the townships, living on public charity: some are at Penetanguishine: and the greater part of those located on their land have received from time to time rations of food, in order to avert "impending starvation." To bring them up from Quebec during the dreadful cholera season of 1832, was a heavy expense to the colony, and now they are likely to become a permanent burthen upon the colonial funds, there being no military funds to which they can be charged.

I make no reflection on the commuting the pensions of these poor men at four instead of seven years' purchase: many of the men I saw did not know what was meant by *commuting their pension:* they thought they merely gave up their pension for four years, and were then to receive it again; they knew nothing of Canada—had never heard of it—had a vague idea that a very fine offer was made, which it would be foolish to refuse. They were like children—which, indeed, disbanded soldiers and sailors usually are.

All that benevolence and prudence *could* suggest, was done for them by Sir John Colborne: he aided them largely from his own purse—himself a soldier and a brave one, as well as a good man—the wrongs and miseries of these poor soldiers wrung his very heart. The strongest remonstrances and solicitations to the heads of the government at home were sent over in their behalf; but there came a change of ministry; the thing once done, could not be undone—redress was nobody's business—the mother country had got rid of a burthen, and it had fallen on Canada; and so the matter ended: that is, as far as it concerned the Treasury and the War-office; but the tragedy has not yet ended *here*. Sir Francis Head, who never can allude to the subject without emotion and indignation, told me, that when he was at Penetanguishine last year, the poor veterans attempted to get up a feeble cheer in his honour, but, in doing so, the half of them fell down. "It was too much for me—too much," added he, with the tears actually in his eyes. As for Sir John Colborne, the least allusion to the subject seemed to give him a twinge of pain.

From this sum of mischief and misery you may subtract a few instances where the men have done better; one of these I had occasion to mention. I have heard of two others, and there may be more, but the general case is as I have stated it.

These were the men who fought our battles in Egypt, Spain, and France! and here is a new page for Alfred de Vigny's "Servitude et Grandeur Militaire!" But do you not think it includes another lesson? That this amount of suffering, and injury, and injustice, can be inflicted from the errors, ignorance, and remoteness of the home government, and that the responsibility apparently rests nowhere—and that nowhere lies redress—seems to me very strange, a very lamentable state of things, and what *ought* not to be.*

* I give the following individual case, noted at the time in my diary:

"*Sept.* 7, 1837.—Called on me Anthony M'Donell, invalided from the 47th, first battalion, to the 12th veteran battalion—located in the twelfth concession of the township of Emily; age 69; twenty-one years in active service; commuted his pension of 14*l*. a year for four years; never knew what commuting meant; received 26*l*. in Ireland, and 13*l*. odd shillings at Quebec; deducting the expense of his voyage, 13*l*. remains due to him from government; does not know where to apply for it—has applied to the commissariat here in vain; *has no friend*; has a daughter aged nineteen, an idiot, and subject to epileptic fits. He brought his daughter with him; the unhappy girl is tall and handsome; the father dare not leave her for a moment; there is no lunatic asylum in Canada to receive her, only the jail, "*and I'll die,*" said the father vehemently, "*before she shall go there.*" He cannot *sell* his land, for present subsistence, because he cannot take out his deed—cannot take out his deed, because he cannot do the duty-work on his land required by law—cannot work, because he cannot leave his poor daughter: he had come to Toronto to beg a few articles of clothing for her. The poor man cried very much, while the childish insensibility and good looks of the daughter were yet more deplorable.

Here is another case of a different kind:—

Dr. Winder, a gentleman who has distinguished himself by writing cleverly in the newspapers here, on what is considered the right side of politics (*i.e.* the support of the British supremacy in the colony,) came out with an order from Lord Bathurst for 500 acres of land, having served in the army twenty years. He was told, on arriving, that his papers were irregular, and that he must have an order from the Commander-in-chief. What is to be done? "Petition the Colonial-office." Will you forward my petition? "You must petition *direct*." The petition was sent—returned in some months as irregular, because not sent through the governor: the ministry changed—there was delay on delay, and at this time (1837) Dr. Winder has not received his grant of land.

Colonel Fitz Gibbon, a very *preux chevalier* of bravery and loyalty, who saved Toronto, on the fourth of December, by placing the pickets before M'Nab came up, is likely to be involved in a similar predicament. The House of Assembly, on meeting, voted him unanimously five thousands acres of the waste government lands, as an acknowledgment of his services. The grant waits for royal confirmation: it is to be hoped it will not wait long.

There is no sense of injustice that would shake the loyalty and principles of such a man as Colonel Fitz Gibbon: like the old Roman, "it were easier to turn the sun from its course, than him from the path of honour;" but all are not like *him*; and the ranks of the disaffected are perpetually recruited in Canada from the ranks of the injured. The commissary told me expressly, that some of these commuted pensioners, who were respectable men, had joined what he called the "Radical set," from a sense of ill treatment.

Our voyageurs had spent the day in various excesses, and next morning were still half tipsy, lazy, and out of spirits, except Le Duc; he was the only one I could persuade to sing, as we crossed Gloucester Bay from Penetanguishine to Coldwater. This bay abounds in sturgeon, which are caught and cured in large quantities by the neighbouring settlers; some weigh ninety and one hundred pounds.

At Matchadash (which signifies "bad and swampy place") we had nearly lost our way among the reeds.

There is a portage here of sixteen miles across the forest to the Narrows, at the head of Lake Simcoe. The canoe and baggage were laid on a cart, and drawn by oxen; the gentlemen walked, as I must also have done, if a Methodist preacher of the neighbourhood had not kindly brought his little wagon and driven me over the portage. We stopped about half-way at his log-hut in the wilderness, where I found his wife, a pretty, refined looking woman, and five or six lovely children, of all ages and sizes. They entertained me with their best, and particularly with delicious preserves, made of the wood-strawberries and raspberries, boiled with the maple sugar.

The country here (after leaving the low swamps) is very rich, and the settlers fast increasing. During the last winter the bears had the audacity to carry off some heifers, to the great consternation of the new settlers, and the wolves did much mischief. I inquired about the Indian settlements at Coldwater and the Narrows; but the accounts were not encouraging. I had been told, as a proof of the advancement of the Indians, that they had here saw-mills and grist-mills. I now learned that they had a saw-mill and a grist-mill built for them, which they never used themselves, but *let out* to the white settlers at a certain rate.

The road through the forest was bordered in many places by raspberry bushes, bearing fruit as fine, and large, and abundant, as any I have seen in our gardens.

In spite of the mosquitoes, my drive was very pleasant; for my companion was good-natured, intelligent, and communicative, and gave me a most interesting, but rather sad, account of his missionary adventures. The road, *as usual*, most detestable. We passed a lovely little lake called Bass

Lake, from the numbers of these fish found in it; and arrived late at the inn at the Narrows. Though much fatigued, I was kept awake nearly the whole night by the sounds of drunken revelry in the room below. Many of the settlers in the neighbourhood are discharged soldiers and half-pay officers, who have received grants of land; and, removed from all social intercourse and all influence of opinion, many have become reckless and habitual drunkards. The only salvation of a man here is to have a wife and children; the poor wife must make up her mind to lead a hard life; but the children are almost *sure* to do well—that is, if they have intelligent parents: it is the very land for the young, and the enterprising. I used to hear parents regret that they could not give what is called a *good* education to their children: but where there are affection and common sense, and a boundless nature round them, and the means of health and subsistence, which (with common industry) all can command here, it seems that education—*i.e.* the development of all the faculties in a direction suited to the country in which they are to exist—comes of course. I saw an example of this in the excellent family of the Magraths of Erindale; but those persons are unfortunate and miserable, and truly pitiable, who come here with habits previously formed, and unable to adapt themselves to an entirely new existence—of such I saw too many. My landlady gave me no agreeable picture of the prevalent habits of the settlers round this place; the riot of which I complained was of nightly occurrence.

Next day we went on a fishing and shooting excursion to Lake Cuchuching, and to see the beautiful rapids of the river Severn, the outlet from these lakes into Lake Huron. If I had not exhausted all my superlatives of delight, I could be eloquent on the charms of this exquisite little lake, and the wild beauty of the rapids. Of our *sport*, I only recollect the massacre of a dozen snakes which were holding a kind of *conversazione* in the hollow of a rocky islet where we landed to dine. The islands in Lake Cuchuching belong to the Indian chief, the Yellow-head; and I understand that he and others of his tribe have petitioned for *legal titles* to their reserved lands. They represent to their Father the governor that their prosperity is retarded from the circumstance of their not having titles to their lands, like their white brethren. They say, "Many of our young men, and some of our chiefs, fear that the time will arrive when our white brethren will possess themselves of our farms: whereas, if our Father the governor would be pleased to grant us titles, we should work with more confidence,"—and they *humbly* entreat, (the original lords of the soil!) as a particular boon, that their "little bits of land" may be secured to their children and posterity for ever.

Next morning we embarked on board the Peter Robinson steamer, and proceeded down Lake Simcoe. This most beautiful piece of water is above forty miles in length, and about twenty in breadth, and is in winter so firmly frozen over, that it is crossed in sledges in every direction. The shores are flat and fertile; and we passed a number of clearings, some very extensive. On a point projecting into the lake, and surrounded by cleared land, a village has been laid out, and some houses built. I went into one of them to rest while they were taking in wood, and found there the works of Shakspeare and Walter Scott, and a good guitar; but the family were absent.

We reached the Holland Landing, at the southern extremity of the lake, about three o'clock, and the rest of our way lay through the Home District, and through some of the finest land and most prosperous estates in Upper Canada. It was a perpetual succession, not of clearings such as I had seen of late, but of well-cultivated farms. The vicinity of the capital, and an excellent road leading to it, (called Yonge Street,) have raised the value of landed property here, and some of the farmers are reputed rich men. Every thing told of prosperity and security: yet all this part of the country was, within a few weeks after, the scene of ill-advised rebellion, of tumult, and *murder!*

Mr. Jarvis gave me an account of an Irish emigrant, a labouring man, who had entered his service some years ago as teamster (or carter:) he was then houseless and penniless. Seven years afterwards the same man was the proprietor of a farm of two hundred acres of cleared and cropped land, on which he could proudly set his foot, and say, "It is mine, and my children's after me!"

At three o'clock in the morning, just as the moon was setting in Lake Ontario, I arrived at the door of my own house in Toronto, having been absent on this wild expedition just two months.

THE AUTHOR

Anna Brownell Jameson was born in Dublin in 1794, the daughter of the artist Denis Brownell Murphy. In 1825 she married Robert Sympson Jameson, who was in 1833 appointed attorney general of Upper Canada. She joined her husband in Toronto in 1836, where she gathered the material for *Winter Studies and Summer Rambles in Canada*, which she published upon her return to England in 1838. Her other books include *Characteristics of Women* (1832), *Visits and* Sketches (1834), and her *magnum opus* in the form of a series of books on art criticism (1841–1861). The chief of these was her four-volume work, *Sacred and Legendary Art*. She died in London, England, in 1860.

THE NEW CANADIAN LIBRARY LIST

n 1. OVER PRAIRIE TRAILS / Frederick Philip Grove
n 2. SUCH IS MY BELOVED / Morley Callaghan
n 3. LITERARY LAPSES / Stephen Leacock
n 4. AS FOR ME AND MY HOUSE / Sinclair Ross
n 5. THE TIN FLUTE / Gabrielle Roy
n 6. THE CLOCKMAKER / Thomas Chandler Haliburton
n 7. THE LAST BARRIER AND OTHER STORIES / Charles G. D. Roberts
n 8. BAROMETER RISING / Hugh MacLennan
n 9. AT THE TIDE'S TURN AND OTHER STORIES / Thomas H. Raddall
n10. ARCADIAN ADVENTURES WITH THE IDLE RICH / Stephen Leacock
n11. HABITANT POEMS / William Henry Drummond
n12. THIRTY ACRES / Ringuet
n13. EARTH AND HIGH HEAVEN / Gwethalyn Graham
n14. THE MAN FROM GLENGARRY /Ralph Connor
n15. SUNSHINE SKETCHES OF A LITTLE TOWN / Stephen Leacock
n16. THE STEPSURE LETTERS / Thomas McCulloch
n17. MORE JOY IN HEAVEN / Morley Callaghan
n18. WILD GEESE / Martha Ostenso
n19. THE MASTER OF THE MILL / Frederick Philip Grove
n20. THE IMPERIALIST / Sara Jeannette Duncan
n21. DELIGHT / Mazo de la Roche
n22. THE SECOND SCROLL / A. M. Klein
n23. THE MOUNTAIN AND THE VALLEY / Ernest Buckler
n24. THE RICH MAN / Henry Kreisel
n25. WHERE NESTS THE WATER HEN / Gabrielle Roy
n26. THE TOWN BELOW / Roger Lemelin
n27. THE HISTORY OF EMILY MONTAGUE / Frances Brooke
n28. MY DISCOVERY OF ENGLAND / Stephen Leacock
n29. SWAMP ANGEL / Ethel Wilson
n30. EACH MAN'S SON / Hugh MacLennan
n31. ROUGHING IT IN THE BUSH / Susanna Moodie
n32. WHITE NARCISSUS / Raymond Knister
n33. THEY SHALL INHERIT THE EARTH / Morley Callaghan
n34. TURVEY / Earle Birney
n35. NONSENSE NOVELS / Stephen Leacock
n36. GRAIN / R. J. C. Stead
n37. LAST OF THE CURLEWS / Fred Bodsworth
n38. THE NYMPH AND THE LAMP / Thomas H. Raddall
n39. JUDITH HEARNE / Brian Moore
n40. THE CASHIER / Gabrielle Roy
n41. UNDER THE RIBS OF DEATH / John Marlyn
n42. WOODSMEN OF THE WEST / M. Allerdale Grainger
n43. MOONBEAMS FROM THE LARGER LUNACY / Stephen Leacock
n44. SARAH BINKS / Paul Hiebert
n45. SON OF A SMALLER HERO / Mordecai Richler
n46. WINTER STUDIES AND SUMMER RAMBLES / Anna Jameson
n47. REMEMBER ME / Edward Meade
n48. FRENZIED FICTION / Stephen Leacock
n49. FRUITS OF THE EARTH / Frederick Philip Grove
n50. SETTLERS OF THE MARSH / Frederick Philip Grove
n51. THE BACKWOODS OF CANADA / Catharine Parr Traill
n52. MUSIC AT THE CLOSE / Edward McCourt
n53. MY REMARKABLE UNCLE / Stephen Leacock

n54. THE DOUBLE HOOK / Sheila Watson
n55. TIGER DUNLOP'S UPPER CANADA / William Dunlop
n56. STREET OF RICHES / Gabrielle Roy
n57. SHORT CIRCUITS / Stephen Leacock
n58. WACOUSTA / John Richardson
n59. THE STONE ANGEL / Margaret Laurence
n60. FURTHER FOOLISHNESS / Stephen Leacock
n61. MARCHBANKS' ALMANACK / Robertson Davies
n62. THE LAMP AT NOON AND OTHER STORIES / Sinclair Ross
n63. THE HARBOUR MASTER / Theodore Goodridge Roberts
n64. THE CANADIAN SETTLER'S GUIDE / Catharine Parr Traill
n65. THE GOLDEN DOG / William Kirby
n66. THE APPRENTICESHIP OF DUDDY KRAVITZ / Mordecai Richler
n67. BEHIND THE BEYOND / Stephen Leacock
n68. A STRANGE MANUSCRIPT FOUND IN A COPPER CYLINDER / James De Mille
n69. LAST LEAVES / Stephen Leacock
n70. THE TOMORROW-TAMER / Margaret Laurence
n71. ODYSSEUS EVER RETURNING / George Woodcock
n72. THE CURE OF ST. PHILIPPE / Francis William Grey
n73. THE FAVOURITE GAME / Leonard Cohen
n74. WINNOWED WISDOM / Stephen Leacock
n75. THE SEATS OF THE MIGHTY / Gilbert Parker
n76. A SEARCH FOR AMERICA / Frederick Philip Grove
n77. THE BETRAYAL / Henry Kreisel
n78. MAD SHADOWS / Marie-Claire Blais
n79. THE INCOMPARABLE ATUK / Mordecai Richler
n80. THE LUCK OF GINGER COFFEY / Brian Moore
n81. JOHN SUTHERLAND: ESSAYS, CONTROVERSIES AND POEMS / Miriam Waddington
n82. PEACE SHALL DESTROY MANY / Rudy Henry Wiebe
n83. A VOICE FROM THE ATTIC / Robertson Davies
n84. PROCHAIN EPISODE / Hubert Aquin
n85. ROGER SUDDEN / Thomas H. Raddall
n86. MIST ON THE RIVER / Hubert Evans
n87. THE FIRE-DWELLERS / Margaret Laurence
n88. THE DESERTER / Douglas LePan
n89. ANTOINETTE DE MIRECOURT / Rosanna Leprohon
n90. ALLEGRO / Felix Leclerc
n91. THE END OF THE WORLD AND OTHER STORIES / Mavis Gallant
n92. IN THE VILLAGE OF VIGER AND OTHER STORIES / Duncan Campbell Scott
n93. THE EDIBLE WOMAN / Margaret Atwood
n94. IN SEARCH OF MYSELF / Frederick Philip Grove
n95. FEAST OF STEPHEN / Robertson Davies
n96. A BIRD IN THE HOUSE / Margaret Laurence
n97. THE WOODEN SWORD / Edward McCourt
n98. PRIDE'S FANCY / Thomas Raddall
n99. OX BELLS AND FIREFLIES / Ernest Buckler
n100. ABOVE GROUND / Jack Ludwig
n101. NEW PRIEST IN CONCEPTION BAY / Robert Traill Spence Lowell
n102. THE FLYING YEARS / Frederick Niven
n103. WIND WITHOUT RAIN / Selwyn Dwedney
n104. TETE BLANCHE / Marie-Claire Blais
n105. TAY JOHN / Howard O'Hagan
n106. CANADIANS OF OLD / Charles G. D. Roberts
n107. HEADWATERS OF CANADIAN LITERATURE / Andrew MacMechan

n108. THE BLUE MOUNTAINS OF CHINA / Rudy Wiebe
n109. THE HIDDEN MOUNTAIN / Gabrielle Roy
n110. THE HEART OF THE ANCIENT WOOD / Charles G. D. Roberts
n111. JEST OF GOD / Margaret Laurence
n112. SELF CONDEMNED / Wyndham Lewis
n113. DUST OVER THE CITY / André Langevin
n114. OUR DAILY BREAD / Frederick Philip Grove
n115. THE CANADIAN NOVEL IN THE TWENTIETH CENTURY / edited by George Woodcock
n116. THE VIKING HEART / Laura Goodman Salverson
n117. DOWN THE LONG TABLE / Earle Birney
n118. GLENGARRY SCHOOL DAYS / Ralph Connor
n119. THE PLOUFFE FAMILY / Roger Lemelin
n120. WINDFLOWER / Gabrielle Roy
n121. THE DISINHERITED / Matt Cohen
n122. THE TEMPTATIONS OF BIG BEAR / Rudy Wiebe
n123. PANDORA / Sylvia Fraser
n124. HOUSE OF HATE / Percy Janes
n125. A CANDLE TO LIGHT THE SUN / Patricia Blondal
n126. THIS SIDE JORDAN / Margaret Laurence
n127. THE RED FEATHERS / T. G. Roberts
n128. I AM MARY DUNNE / Brian Moore
n129. THE ROAD PAST ALTAMONT / Gabrielle Roy
n130. KNIFE ON THE TABLE / Jacques Godbout
n131. THE MANAWAKA WORLD OF MARGARET LAURENCE / Clara Thomas
n132. CONSIDER HER WAYS / Frederick Philip Grove
n133. HIS MAJESTY'S YANKEES / Thomas Raddall
n134. JEAN RIVARD / Antoine Gérin-Lajoie
n135. BOGEL CORBET / John Galt
n136. A CHOICE OF ENEMIES / Mordecai Richler
n137. ESSAYS ON CANADA / E. K. Brown
n138. THE MASTER'S WIFE / Andrew McPhail
n139. THE CRUELEST MONTH / Ernest Buckler
n140. THE ATONEMENT OF ASHLEY MORDEN / Fred Bodsworth
n141. WILD ANIMALS I HAVE KNOWN / Ernest Seaton
n142. SCANN / Robert Harlow
n143. A CANADIAN POETICS / A. J. H. Smith
n144. CRACKPOT / Adele Wiseman
n145. SAWBONES MEMORIAL / Sinclair Ross
n146. THE DIVINERS / Margaret Laurence
n147. HIGH BRIGHT BUGGY WHEELS / Luella Creighton
n148. BIG LONELY / James Bacque
n149. WOODEN HUNTERS / Matt Cohen
n150. GOD'S SPARROWS / Philip Child
n151. THE OUTLANDER / Germaine Guèvremont
n152. THE GREAT COMIC BOOK HEROES AND OTHER ESSAYS BY MORDECAI RICHLER / edited by Robert Fulford
n153 BEAUTIFUL LOSERS/Leonard Cohen
n154 THE EMPEROR OF ICE-CREAM/Brian Moore
n155 GARDEN IN THE WIND and ENCHANTED SUMMER/Gabrielle Roy
n156 THE SCORCHED-WOOD PEOPLE/Rudy Wiebe
n157 THE LOST SALT GIFT OF BLOOD/Alistair MacLeod
n158 LORD NELSON TAVERN/Ray Smith